5

conversations
you must have
with your
daughter

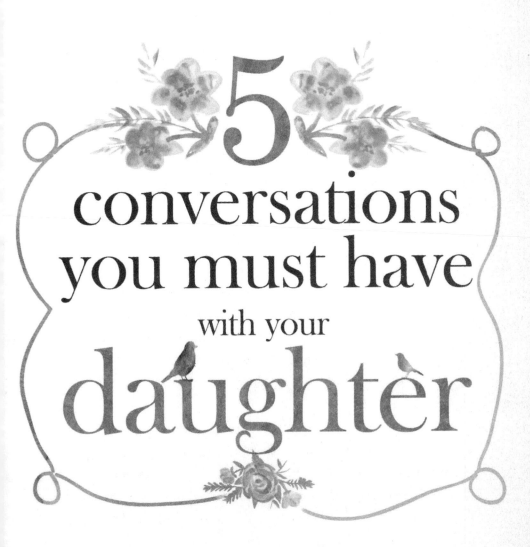

5
conversations
you must have
with your
daughter

vicki courtney

PUBLISHING GROUP
Nashville, Tennessee

978-1-4336-9161-4

Published by B&H Publishing Group
Nashville, Tennessee

Mass custom edition.

Author is represented by the literary agency of
Alive Communications, Inc., 7680 Goddard Street, Suite 200,
Colorado Springs, Colorado 80920.

1 2 3 4 5 • 19 18 17 16

To my daughter, Paige

For eighteen years, you have listened to my never-ending sermonettes, teachable moments, and soapbox rants over the culture's negative influences. Now it's time for me to talk less and pray more, loosen my grip, and ask God to tighten His. I have no doubts you will soar . . . I love you, sweet girl.

Also, to Paige's closest friends, who by default of being her closest friends have had to endure a teachable moment, or two, or three . . . or a hundred: Jesi, Lauren, Jessica, Kelti, Taralah, Kaitlin and Jennifer (J'niece). I adore you and count you as my own!

Acknowledgments

To my husband, Keith: Thank you for your continued support and willingness to read and edit some of my chapters on top of your already busy full-time job. Three more years, and we're empty-nesters. Can you believe it? I can't wait to grow old with you and sit in our new rockers on the front porch.

To my children: Ryan, Paige, and Hayden: I know it's not always been easy having a mom who speaks and writes on teen culture . . . especially during your teen years. You have been real troopers! Your dad and I are having a blast watching you mature in the faith. Watch out, world!

To my friends at B&H: It has been such a joy to partner with you in this project. Thank you for believing sincerely in the message.

To my agent, Lee Hough: I am so blessed to have you in my corner. You are the best!

To Linda Attaway: Thank you for lending your talents to read this manuscript and make edits before it went to my publisher. I am forever grateful for your kindness . . . and your friendship.

To Barbara Andrews: Thank you, sweet friend, for loving on my daughter and being a mentor to her in her senior year. The mother/daughter relationship you had with Lauren was an inspiration to all. She would be so proud of you.

To Janet Watson: We did it! We got our girls through high school and by the time you read this, we will have moved them into their respective dorms. It wasn't always easy, but we sure made some great memories along the way. It was so nice having you along for the ride.

To my VirtueAlert.com blog readers: Thank you for participating in surveys related to the research for this book. I hope our real-life paths will cross someday so I can hug your necks in person.

To my Lord and Savior, Jesus Christ: Thank You for allowing me any part in pointing others to Your goodness and glory. My heart is forever Yours.

Contents

Introduction

Introductions are kind of a big deal to me. For that reason, rarely do I turn an introduction in when I submit the rest of the manuscript to my publisher. Rather, I wait until the final stage of editing, when the book comes back to me one last time (generally weeks shy of going to the printer). In order to set the tone and attitude of the book, I read it cover to cover, in one sitting. I know it's going to be the first thing you read, so I want it to be the last thing I write. I share this little detail with you in order that you might better appreciate the unbelievable irony of my to-do list for this week:

- ☑ Write introduction for 5 *Conversations*
- ☑ Go over dorm packing list w/ Paige
- ☑ Find pet care re: college drop-off

What weird timing. I thought it was weird enough that I wrote this book during her entire senior year. I was writing the book in between watching her cheer at Varsity games and pep rallies for the last time. I was writing this book when she received her acceptance letter in the mail from her number one college choice. I was writing this book in between shopping for a homecoming dress and a prom dress. I was writing this book during her first-ever dating relationship. I was writing this book while planning a dinner for her eighteenth birthday. And now, here I sit in my favorite writing chair writing this introduction, while she is upstairs taking an inventory of the contents in her bedroom and putting things aside in a "take-to-college" pile. Can someone hand me a tissue, please?

By the time you hold this book in your hands, my husband and I will have packed up our baby girl's belongings and trekked more than eight hundred miles, crossing four state lines to move her into her dorm room. Mind you, she has never been away from home for longer than a week. Oh, I know she'll come home for visits and summer vacations and that brings me some comfort. But the truth is, she is not likely to *return home* and take up residence in her room again. Just down the hall from me. Where I know she is safe and sound. I've already done a college drop-off with her older brother, so I know better than to think she is headed to camp for four years. Did I mention that she's never been away from home for longer than a week? Ugh.

And yet, in this twisted sense of irony, here stands my girl on the precipice of college D-Day (drop-off day) as I do a final read on a book called 5 *Conversations You Must Have with Your Daughter*. I am left to wonder if I have met the challenge of the very subtitle of this book: *"From cradle to college: Tell your daughters the truth about life before they believe the culture's lies."* Did I say enough? Do enough? Teach her enough? Prepare her enough to live on her own? Did I equip her enough in dating matters to avoid the Bozos who will, no doubt, cross her path? Remind her enough that God has a different standard of beauty? Love her enough? Model my faith enough? Did I point her to Christ enough?

Isn't it a mother's nature to always wonder if we've *done enough?* Fortunately I am reminded that God is *more than enough* to make up for my parenting insufficiencies along the way. When it comes to parenting my daughter, the bulk of my job is over. Wait, maybe I should add that to my list, just for the sheer pleasure of putting a check beside it!

☑ Fulfill eighteen-year-parenting assignment from
   God re: Paige

It's tough to raise a girl in today's culture. I have never been one to sugarcoat the facts and sometimes this book will make you squirm. I have had the five conversations contained in this book with my own daughter. Over and over again. The basic premise behind these conversations is that they are *ongoing* conversations. They should start when your daughter is young and continue through the years. You don't stop talking when she starts pulling away or rolling her eyes. In fact, you step them up. And you pray, pray, pray, and lean on God for strength, wisdom, and discernment. You can't do this in your own strength—You need the Lord's help. Before you know it, my friend, it will be your turn to pack your girl up for college or send her off into the working world. My sincerest prayer is that when that time comes, you, too, will feel an overall sense of satisfaction over your eighteen-year-parenting assignment. God is not looking for perfect mothers to raise perfect daughters. He's looking for imperfect mothers who are raising imperfect daughters in an imperfect world . . . and desperately dependant on a perfect God for the results.

—Vicki Courtney

CONVERSATION 1

You Are More Than
the Sum of Your Parts

CHAPTER ONE

Pretty Packaging

H ave you ever been lured by pretty packaging? Product manufacturers who aim for successful sales know the importance of packaging. Further they know that consumers make as many as 70 percent of their buying decisions in the store and can face up to 100,000 items that bid for their attention.[1] Whether it's a pack of gum, a tube of toothpaste, or a bag of chips, you can bet that countless dollars and hours have been invested into analyzing everything from the target audience to color palettes and shelf placement. The end goal, of course, is for the product to stand out on the shelf and, above all, to get picked up by the consumer and scanned at the checkout.

Now, what if I told you that your little girl is also a product? Her brand managers work around the clock to make sure she knows exactly what it will take to get noticed. If she is to catch the eye of her target audience, the packaging must be perfect. And by *perfect* I mean "flawless." By the time she celebrates her twelfth birthday, she will have seen an estimated 77,546 commercials.[2] Add to it the images she sees daily from magazines, billboards, and the Internet, and you can be certain that by the time she blows out sixteen candles, she will be clear of her role as defined by culture. Over and over again she will be told to lose weight, tone up, dress provocatively, and flaunt it. Pure and simple, she is an object for the male viewing pleasure. She is bidding for male attention among a sea of contenders. And her target audience is picky. He, too, has been inundated with images of picture-perfect women. He has zero tolerance for flat chests, chunky thighs, cellulite, blemishes, split ends, or facial wrinkles. Why should he settle for less than a PhotoShop best? He has come to believe that the airbrushed images are the standard of beauty.

More than three-quarters of girls and young women admit to partaking in unhealthy activities when they feel badly about their bodies.

Your daughter has been duped, and it's up to you to expose the lie. If she conforms her identity to the culture's narrow definition of beauty, you can be sure that it will permeate every corner of her life from this moment forward. Ninety-three percent of girls and young women report feeling anxiety or stress about some aspect of their looks when getting ready in the morning. More than three-quarters of girls and young women admit to partaking in unhealthy activities when they feel badly about their bodies. Fifty-eight percent of girls describe themselves in negative terms, including words like *disgusting* and *ugly*, when feeling badly about themselves. Nearly four out of ten engage in unhealthy eating behaviors, such as anorexia or bulimia.[3]

Don't be fooled. Your daughter will be exposed to the lie. Most will fall for it. Some will show outward manifestations when the foundation begins to crack. Others will suffer in silence. They will wear a smile on their face and appear unbothered by the pressure to measure up to this narrow definition of beauty. Their secret will be safe for now. The self-loathing they feel will only be revealed in private when they step out of the shower and catch a glimpse of themselves in the bathroom mirror. Or step on the scales at the doctor's office. Or stand in the department store dressing room as they wrestle into the size they wish they were. Or sit by a pool with a girlfriend who caught the lifeguard's eye when she strolled by.

Think about it. When was the last time you picked up a fashion magazine and read a subtitle that focused on inner beauty? Whether its advice on fashion, dieting, or pleasing men in the bedroom, the message to our girls is loud and clear. The packaging is of utmost importance. And the reward for a pretty package? A wink perhaps or a catcall from an onlooker. Some may even be labeled "hot" or "sexy." The grand prize is that the "package" would succeed in becoming the object of the male desire. Isn't that what it's really all about? Here we are almost four decades past the women's movement, and yet women have never been more objectified than they are today.

A Sad State of Affairs

I was reminded of this recently after writing a post on my blog about the Vanessa Hudgens scandal. In case you don't remember the story, Ms. Hudgens is the *High School Musical* starlet who had nude pictures leaked to the Web by an unknown source. Many news links offered public forums where their readers could post their own comments regarding the scandal. I was nauseous as I read comments from men both young and old who analyzed her each and every body part.

Some commented on her breast size, and others expressed disappointment that she had not waxed her bikini line (and more). Mind you, several of the pictures were rumored to have been taken when she was a mere sixteen years old. Over and over again, men would say, "I would do her," some even elaborating in detail. These are not porn sites, moms and dads. Many of these are reputable news sites that fail to monitor or censor reader comments. It offers us a glimpse into the fallout from a hypersexualized, porn-riddled culture.

Don't be fooled. Your sons and daughters have been exposed (or will be exposed) to this filth at some point. Perhaps they are among the 7.08 million viewers who tuned in to watch the 2007 MTV Video Music Awards for Britney Spears's rumored comeback performance.[4] Or if they missed it, perhaps they were among the 1.5 million plus viewers who have watched it after the fact on YouTube in the days that followed. Suffice it to say, this was no comeback performance. In fact, when I watched it, I saw much more than a girl who stumbled around on stage in little more than her bra and panties and forgot the words to the song. I saw a girl, whose fame was built on the objectification of her body beginning at the age of fifteen, who had since become a poster child for all that can go wrong when your worth is based on the sum of your parts. Oh sure, it can be argued that she welcomed and even encouraged the attention, but in all fairness, did she realize at the time that the same male admirers who once hung her poster on the wall would turn on her the minute she gained a pound?

Am I the only one who wonders if her struggles with mental instability have anything to do with believing she is, in fact, nothing more than the sum of her parts? Now that her parts aren't adding up like they used to, she is left wondering who she is and if she matters. In addition, I found it particularly disturbing when reading the comments about her performance posted on YouTube and other gossip news sites that much of the consensus seemed to be that she was "fat." In reality, most women would be so fortunate to look like she did so soon after delivering two babies. This is yet another example of a culture that has imposed a narrow definition of beauty, which does not allow for the natural effects of child-bearing or aging. Women are expected to return to their prechild-birth bodies that show no evidence whatsoever of the beauty of motherhood. The culture's definition of beauty does not tolerate stretch marks and excess skin that might cover up once firm six-pack abs. And the reward, you may wonder, to the woman who is able to birth multiple children, hire a chef to whip up low-fat meals, and rely on her trainer to whip her back into shape? If you are a celebrity mom who accomplishes such a feat, you might be featured on TMZ.com (a popular celebrity gossip site) under their category of "Hot Mamas." A particularly "hot mama" may even be labeled as a "MILF" (Mother I'd like to f***) by TMZ or readers who relish the opportunity to sum up the featured celebrity's body parts and submit their analysis. There are no shortage of comments from perverts ranging from "I'd do her" to "I'd tap that."[5] What a sad and pathetic state of affairs. And all the while, our daughters (and sons) are watching and taking notes.

A Narrow Definition of Beauty

Moms, can you relate to the pressure your daughter feels? I'm betting you can. And trust me, you are not alone. A study commissioned by the Dove Foundation found that 57 percent of all women strongly agree that "the attributes of female beauty have become very narrowly defined in today's world," and 68 percent strongly agree that "the media and advertising set an unrealistic standard of beauty that most women can't ever achieve."[6] Are you angry about the constant bombardment of this skewed definition of beauty? I know I am. In fact, I'm fighting mad, and it's one of the driving forces behind the message of this book. Enough is enough. If this chapter incites you to anger, that's OK. Oftentimes, anger is the stimulus to action.

The challenge to redefine beauty is nothing new. God cautioned His people long ago against judging a person based on the sum of their parts. When Samuel, the prophet, was called by God to anoint the next king to follow Saul, God chastised him for assuming that David's older brother, Eliab, might be next in line to the throne based on his handsome appearance. In 1 Samuel 16:6, Samuel took one look at Eliab and thought, "Surely the LORD's anointed stands here before the LORD." The verse that follows reveals God's standard for judging beauty when He tells Samuel, "Do not consider his appearance or his height, for I have rejected him. The LORD does not look at the things man looks at. Man looks at the outward appearance, but the LORD looks at the heart" (1 Sam. 16:7).

Together we are going to tackle the culture's lies in order that you might initiate some necessary conversations and arm your daughter with the truth about beauty—God's truth. Whether your daughter has already built a foundation on the culture's lies or is just beginning to be exposed to the brainwashing, trust me, the battle is not lost. Where God is present, there is always hope. Only by speaking up and addressing the lies head on will we equip our daughters. Our silence, on the other hand, will endorse the culture's lies and leave them with the impression that they amount to nothing more than the sum of their parts. Our daughters need to know that God's standard for beauty is the only standard that matters. Amazingly, His standard used to be the culture's accepted standard. Today we are witnessing the results

> Our daughters need to know that God's standard for beauty is the only standard that matters.

of a culture that long ago took its eyes off God as the standard for beauty, goodness, and morality.

Vintage Beauty Secrets, Circa 1890

Can you imagine opening up your daughter's diary and reading "Dear Diary, help me to be pretty on the inside." That's what a mother in the late 1800s might be likely to find. Joan Jacobs Brumberg, author of *The Body Project*, researched girls' diaries and journals from the late 1800s to early 1900s to track the shift in attitudes regarding appearance. She found that "before World War I, girls rarely mentioned their bodies in terms of strategies for self-improvement or struggles for personal identity." She stated, "When girls in the nineteenth century thought about ways to improve themselves, they almost always focused on their internal character and how it was reflected in outward behavior. In 1882, the personal agenda of an adolescent diarist read: 'Resolved, not to talk about myself or feelings. To think before speaking. To work seriously. To be self restrained in conversation and actions. Not to let my thoughts wander. To be dignified. Interest myself more in others.'"[7]

Can you imagine how the diaries of today's teen girls might read? I'm convicted enough at the thought of how mine might read in comparison. No doubt, the emphasis on inner beauty is long forgotten. In fact, most girls likely aren't even aware that a time ever existed when a young lady focused on internal attributes. Interestingly, Brumberg noted that girls from the nineteenth century were discouraged from showing too much attention to appearance—to do so would be vanity. The book noted that "character was built on attention to self-control, service to others, and belief in God."[8] One can't help but wonder if girls from the nineteenth century were familiar with the wisdom of Proverbs 31:30 that counsels, "Charm is deceptive, and beauty is fleeting; but a woman who fears the LORD is to be praised." No doubt, becoming a woman who fears the Lord was the end goal of women in the nineteenth century. In a nutshell they prized virtue over vanity.

Today the tables have turned. The Dove Foundation survey mentioned above found that 60 percent of women strongly agreed that "society expects women to enhance their physical attractiveness." Fifty-nine percent strongly agreed that "physically attractive women are more valued by men." Finally, 76 percent strongly agreed that they wished that female beauty was portrayed in the media as being made up of more than just physical attractiveness.[9] It sounds to me like women would like to see beauty become more about virtue and less about vanity.

A century later the word *virtue* is long forgotten and certainly not part of the average girl's vocabulary. So when and how, exactly, did the shift from virtue to vanity occur? Believe it or not, your bathroom mirror can be partially to blame. In *The Body Project*, Brumberg stated, "When the mirror became a staple of the American middle-class home at the end of the nineteenth century, attention to adolescent acne escalated, as did sales of products for the face. Until then, pimples were primarily a tactile experience, at least for the girl who had them. But that all changed in the late 1800s with the widespread adoption in middle-class homes of a bathroom sink with running water and a mirror hung above it." She further noted that "mirrors play a critical role in the way American girls have assessed their own faces and figures."[10]

As mirrors became popularized, women were able to scrutinize and compare their features with the women they saw in movies and magazines, not to mention one another. In the 1920s, American women began to take an interest in cosmetics. From facial powders to rouge, lipstick, and even eyelash curlers, women flocked to the local drugstores to stock up on these beauty accoutrements. The flapper movement further boosted sales of cosmetics among women and especially teenage girls. Blumberg noted that "sales of compacts (small handheld mirrors with a compartment for powder) soared because they allowed women to scrutinize and 'reconstruct' the face almost anywhere, in a moment's notice."[11]

Shortly thereafter, home scales became available, and managing weight became a preoccupation among young women. Until then, the only place a young woman could weigh herself was the drugstore or county fair. Prior to that, dieting and exercise were virtually unheard of, and again, would have been considered a measure of vanity. In fact, I was shocked to discover in Brumberg's book that when young women in the late 1800s left home, they would often write their mothers and speak of healthy weight gain and voracious eating habits. It was almost considered a curse to be slender! Slender girls were thought to be unhealthy and subject to worries of infertility. The ability to bear healthy children was of far greater importance than looking svelte in a swimsuit. As mirrors became more prevalent and the flapper movement gained momentum in the 1920s, women began to express worry over gaining weight, and soon after dieting or "food restriction" became a common topic. The shift from virtue to vanity has been a runaway train ever since.

True Reflections

Stop for a minute and imagine what life might be like without easy access to mirrors and scales. I, for one, stopped weighing myself some years ago in an effort to deconstruct the culture's lie that my happiness is dependent on a certain number on the scale. Having struggled in my teen and college years with an eating disorder,

I had cultivated the bad habit of weighing daily, sometimes multiple times within the day. Should the number exceed my defined range of acceptable by even a mere pound, it set the tone of my entire day. Now my focus is on looking healthy rather than stepping on the scale and allowing it to have the final say.

I am certainly not suggesting that we gather up our mirrors and line them up for target practice and toss our scales into the dumpster, but I am questioning the impact they have had on body image among women. Years ago I spoke to a group of young women who were in a sorority at a large university. One of the officers who had invited me had heard my story of misdefined worth in my own college years. She specifically asked that I share about my own experience with an eating disorder as many of the girls living in the sorority house were suffering from eating disorders that ranged from starving themselves to bulimia. In fact, so serious was the issue that they were experiencing plumbing problems due to the pipes prematurely corroding or the toilets stopping up from all the forced vomiting.

When I arrived at the sorority house on the evening I was scheduled to speak, she gave me a quick tour of the house. Along the way I couldn't help but notice that there were mirrors everywhere. Entire walls had been turned into mirrors in the large meeting room and in the living area. In addition, full-length mirrors were staggered up and down the hallways and along the grand stairwell. When I made a comment about the mirrors being everywhere, she quickly replied, "Why do you think so many of our girls are starving themselves and throwing up? The mirrors serve as a constant reminder that they can never measure up." At that moment I longed for the mirrorless days of the late 1800s, a time when virtue was considered beauty and vanity was considered sin. While it might not be possible to do away with mirrors, it is possible to do away with some of the expectations women have when they see their reflections in the mirrors.

CHAPTER TWO

The Size Demise and the Weight Debate

O n a recent afternoon while shopping with my daughter, I waited outside a dressing room while she tried on some jeans. In the dressing room next to her, a young lady yelled out to her friend, "Oh-em-gee! I am so fat! I can't fit into these size zeros. Will you go get me a size two?" Seriously, I wanted to crawl under the door of that dressing room and feed the girl a cheeseburger. I prayed my daughter had ignored the whole interchange, but chances are it became yet another chink in the armor of the body image battle that wages war within the souls of most women, young and old alike.

Rather than logically deduce that statements like the one above are the product of the culture's narrow definition of beauty, most girls within hearing range will instead glance at themselves in the mirror and feel disgust and shame. One survey found that by age thirteen, 53 percent of American girls are unhappy with their bodies, and by age seventeen 78 percent are dissatisfied.[1] If we are to counter the culture's lies regarding body image, we must first go to the root of the problem and address body shape. I am talking about the God-given body shape your daughter was born with rather than the hourglass ideal the media insists she should have.

> By age thirteen, 53 percent of American girls are unhappy with their bodies, and by age seventeen 78 percent are dissatisfied.

Geometry 101

Amazingly, a recent study found that the hourglass figure is the least dominant shape of women, having made up only 8 percent of the 6,318 U.S. women that were scanned for the study. The study further found that the hourglass shape almost does not exist in women larger than a size eight.[2] Keep in mind that the average woman is 5 feet 3.8 inches and weighs 163 pounds.[3] The same study found that the garment industry assumes that the hourglass figure is the dominant shape of American women and designs their clothing accordingly. Because of this misconception, many women are unable to find clothes designed to flatter their body shape, and as a result, they struggle to make peace with their God-given body shape. In fact, 46 percent of women were found to have more of a rectangular shape, 21 percent were spoon shaped, and 14 percent were shaped more like an inverted triangle.[4]

Putting the geometry lesson aside, imagine a world where there were no premanufactured sizes. A world used to exist over a century ago when clothing was made at home. In *The Body Project*,

Blumberg noted, "In general, mass-produced clothing fostered autonomy in girls because it took matters of style and taste outside the dominion of the mother, who had traditionally made and supervised a girl's wardrobe. . . . So long as clothing was made at home, the dimensions of the garment could be adjusted to the particular body intended to wear it. But with store-bought clothes, the body had to fit instantaneously into standard sizes that were constructed from a pattern representing a norm. When clothing failed to fit the body, particularly a part as intimate as the breasts, young women were apt to perceive that there was something wrong with their bodies."[5]

The garment industry cannot bear the blame alone for the poor body image experienced by most young women. Let's not forget those rice-cake-eating runway models who weigh 23 percent less than the average woman. Consider this: the average runway model is 5 feet 11 inches and weighs 120 pounds. Wait, did I say she eats rice cakes? Strike that. Make that lettuce leaves. The average American teen girl on the other hand, is 5 feet 3.8 inches and weighs 134.5 pounds.[6] Ironically, the average American girl is closer to the ideal weight range, yet she aspires to look like the models. In fact, in a 1995 study, middle-class white girls defined perfection as 5 feet 7 inches tall and 110 pounds.[7]

As time passes, the standards change, becoming increasingly unrealistic and more difficult to attain. Mary Pipher, author of *Reviving Ophelia*, reported that in 1950 the White Rock Mineral Water girl was 5 feet 4 inches tall and weighed 140 pounds. Today, she stands 5 feet 10 inches tall and weighs only 110.[8] A recent study that examined the effect of teen-targeted television on teenage viewers concluded that "as in most of television, these shows tend to cast svelte, attractive females and, to a lesser extent, handsome and 'buff' males. In terms of body type, *no* heavier-than-average main teenage characters appeared on these programs."[9]

We'll talk about the dangers of fashion magazines in more depth later in this section, but we certainly can't deny the part they play in fostering a negative body image among girls. Dr. Susie Orbach (psychotherapist, London School of Economics) has discovered that spending just three minutes looking at fashion magazines lowers the self-esteem of 80 percent of women.[10] On the heels of the Dove Campaign, *Seventeen* magazine is apparently doing some damage control by initiating a "Body Peace" project whose aim is to get girls to "stop obsessing over thinness and criticizing their own figures." *Seventeen* editor Ann Shoket said, "This is not about looking good. It's about feeling great about your body no matter what shape it is. It's hard for young girls to navigate this. Tabloids publish reports about how many ounces celebrities gain," she says. "Girls have no barometer of what's normal and healthy."[11] Really? The tabloids? Do you think *Seventeen* might also need to own some of the blame? I can't help but find this new initiative just a tad hypocritical. Why don't they just nix the anorexic-looking models in all their ads who look like one gust of wind would blow them over to the next zip code and get some realistic-looking girls to take their places? Sorry to sound so skeptical, but it sounds like an attempt to garner a little positive PR.

We can't just lay blame on the garment industry, magazines, and the runway models for our body image issues. Let's not forget that Barbie gal. I recently read that if Barbie's measurements were projected to life-size, they would be 38–18–34, which is not a figure found in nature. If she were a real woman, she would have to walk on all fours because of her unrealistic proportions. But hey, do you remember playing with the "Happy to be me" doll? I'm serious. It was a real doll introduced in the 1990s in an attempt to help girls see a more realistic body shape. Unfortunately, the dolls were a flop, and the company went kaput. The truth is, most girls preferred playing with a doll that had an unrealistic body shape rather than one that had a figure that more resembled the general population of women. But before I call for a Barbie bonfire, let me say that I logged plenty of hours playing with Barbies and don't recall ever thinking, *Wow, I wish I had her bod.* I do remember thinking, *Wow, I wish I had her Corvette.* For the record, I didn't get either.

Body Development and the Impact on Body Image

Ginny Olson, author of the book, Teenage Girls: Exploring Issues Adolescent Girls Face and Strategies to Help Them, states that girls who develop much earlier than their peers usually end up with a poor self-image compared to those girls who develop later. In addition, girls who mature early are more likely to have a negative view of their bodies and to suffer from eating disorders and substance abuse. The book states that one reason for this may be that a girl who physically looks like a woman is often treated by adults and older peers based on her looks rather than how old she actually is. She is truly a little girl trapped in a woman's body. Another reason is that the earlier she matures, the more likely she will get attention from boys, oftentimes even older boys. Again, because of her young age, she is not emotionally prepared to deal with that type of attention.[12]

If your daughter is an early bloomer, do what you can to protect her from the attention of older boys. Discuss openly with her the findings above and make sure she feels comfortable coming to you with any frustrations she may have. You may have to check in with her and ask her some specific questions since girls tend to be private about their feelings associated with body development.

> **I**f your daughter is an early bloomer, do what you can to protect her from the attention of older boys.

Most importantly, make sure your daughter dresses appropriately and wears clothing that reflects her age. Girls (of any age) who dress immodestly tend to draw the wrong kind of attention from the boys. Allowing a little girl to dress this way can invite trouble.

On the other hand, the book found that late-maturing girls often get impatient with their body development. However, as a whole, they tend to be much more satisfied with their looks than girls who develop early. When they hit adolescence, even though it's later in the game, they are usually taller and leaner than their peers and have a better body image. Grade-school girls tend to be confident about their bodies and don't spend much time thinking about their bodies or comparing their shape to others. The only exception to this finding is if the girl portrays an extreme such as being the tallest, shortest, heaviest, or smallest when compared to her peers.[13] If your daughter exhibits one of the above extremes, be sensitive to her struggles and establish an open dialogue with her.

My own daughter was a late bloomer, and while she became frustrated at times about looking more little-girlish than womanly in her early high school years, she emerged with an overall healthy body image. Perhaps most valuable is the fact that she escaped much of the fallout that comes with early attention from boys. If your daughter is a late bloomer, rejoice and remind her of the benefits along the way. Be aware that she may feel frustrated at times and may even harbor some fears that she will never develop. Regardless of whether your daughter is an early or a late bloomer, keep the lines of communication open and reassure her of God's perfect timing.

One Diet Shy of the Perfect Body

I recently had a mother e-mail me for advice on how to deal with a painful situation involving her middle-school-aged daughter. She shared how some mean girls at her daughter's Christian private school posted her daughter's picture on one of the social-networking sites and invited their friends to vote on whether they thought she was fat. Of course, anything that mixes middle school, mean girls, and the Internet is not likely to have a happy ending.

Mom told me that her daughter fell in the upper-end of her suggested weight range and that most of the women in her family had a bigger bone structure. She said that her daughter was involved in sports and that up until this account of Internet bullying had been comfortable with her body shape. The most important piece of information the mother offered was that the pediatrician viewed her daughter's weight as normal and did not consider her overweight. Even so, the mother's question was, "Should I put her on a diet and help her lose weight so she isn't teased in the future?"

For a minute I thought about replying, "Absolutely, and while you're at it, be sure to take her in for a boob job and some lipo. That should do the trick." Excuse me? This is the perfect example of a parent encouraging her child to lean on the culture when it comes to defining beauty, even if the culture is way off base. Perhaps a better solution would be for that mom to sit her daughter down and remind her of Paul's counsel in Romans 12:2: "Do not conform any longer to the pattern of this world, but be transformed by the renewing of your mind. Then you will be able to test and approve what God's will is—his good, pleasing and perfect will." As a bonus she might also remind her of Galatians 1:10: "Am I now trying to win the approval of men, or of God? Or am I trying to please men? If I were still trying to please men, I would not be a servant of Christ." Times will change, as will attitudes regarding what constitutes beauty and, furthermore, a healthy weight range.

Your daughters are growing up in a culture that is obsessed with weight. Often we hear about the dangers of eating disorders among our girls, and certainly the issue is not to be minimized. Joan Jacobs Brumberg in *Fasting Girls: The Emergence of Anorexia Nervosa as a*

Modern Disease puts the number of anorexics at 5 to 10 percent of all American girls and women.[14] Dr. Charles A. Murkovsky of Gracie Square Hospital in New York City, an eating disorder specialist, says that 20 percent of American college women binge and purge on a regular basis. Kim Chernin in *The Hungry Self* suggests that at least half the women on campuses in the United States suffer at some time from bulimia or anorexia.[15]

> More than 43 percent of twelve- to fifteen-year-old girls have been told by their physicians that they're overweight.

However, there is also a flip side. More than 43 percent of twelve- to fifteen-year-old girls have been told by their physicians that they're overweight. The number of overweight adolescents in the U.S. has tripled since 1980. It certainly doesn't help that the average child is exposed to more than forty thousand television ads a year, and the majority are for food products and target young people. Add to this the decrease in physical activity, and we have a major problem.[16]

Of course, the exploding diet industry is all too happy to help. The number of diet-related articles rose 70 percent from 1968 to 1984.[17] Americans spend more than $30 billion a year on diet products.[18] Additionally, researchers found that 40 percent of girls in first through fifth grades reported that they were trying to lose weight.[19] Young girls say that they are more afraid of becoming fat than they are of cancer, nuclear war, or losing their parents.[20] I recently surveyed fifth- and sixth-grade girls and among many questions asked, "What is one worry you have about moving on to middle school?" Of course, I received countless responses related to "too much homework" and "not being able to find my class," but nothing prepared me for the number of answers I got from girls who were worried about "getting fat."

What exactly is the balance when talking to our daughters about dieting and nutrition? On the one hand we want them to steer clear of eating disorders, but on the other we don't want them to experience the dangers of being overweight. It's a tricky balance. Our goal should be to educate our girls to the dangers of both extremes. Our emphasis should not be placed on achieving a target weight range but rather on developing healthy eating habits and exercising on a regular basis. Which begs the question: Is a healthy diet really a diet? No! When we stop looking at these diet plans (eating the foods that are good for us in smaller, more reasonable quantities) as quick fixes and start viewing them as a way of life, we win, and our daughters win. Here's the way I see it: We can talk to our daughters about the dangers of eating disorders and/or being overweight, or we can both talk and act. In doing so, you provide a solution by defeating both extremes, and you increase the odds that they will carry their healthy habits into their adult years.

I don't want to appear to be oversimplifying the solution, and I don't claim to be a nutrition expert. In fact, my children were fed far too much junk food, and were it not for the fact that we are a small-boned family with a big metabolism, we'd all be in a heap o' trouble. I am just as attached to my grande vanilla lattes and cookies and cream ice cream as the next guy. I, too, am learning as I go and working to improve in this area of health and nutrition. In the meantime, allow me to share a few practical tips on how you can help your daughter have a balanced perspective on dieting and nutrition.

Tips to Helping Your Daughter Have a Positive Body Image

1. Give your daughter positive messages that she is beautiful and attractive. In *Teenage Girls: Exploring Issues Adolescent Girls*

Face and Strategies to Help Them, author Ginny Olson states that "mothers especially have a clear impact on their daughter's body image. Girls who have strong and healthy relationships with their mothers are more likely to have a higher sense of self-confidence and a lower incidence of eating disorders."[21]

2. Mothers, watch what you say about your own bodies! Darlene Atkins, the director of the Eating Disorders Clinic at Children's National Medical Center in Washington states, "Sadly, mothers especially are often very critical of their own weight and shape, and their girls absorb that."[22]

> Make the focus in your home nutrition rather than weight loss.

3. Make the focus in your home nutrition rather than weight loss. In the article, "For Teens, Obesity No Laughing Matter," Atkins advocated making home into a "safe zone," primarily by emphasizing feeding one's body in a healthy way, so that it functions at a healthy level—not by dwelling on restrictive dieting. To further support the need to back up our talk with action, Kay Abrams, a clinical psychologist and eating disorders expert, says, "Live by your actions and your lifestyle. Don't lecture and talk about weight all the time. Just change."[23]

4. Never tease your daughter about weight! According to new research from the University of Minnesota, teasing adolescents about weight—especially if the teasing comes from family members—can play a big role in future weight problems. The study found that girls who were teased about their weight were about twice as likely to be overweight five years later as other girls who weren't. In addition, they were also about 1.5 times more likely to engage in binge eating and use extreme weight-control behaviors, like purging or abuse of laxatives, diuretics, or diet pills. Even more

disturbing, the study found that almost half of the overweight girls surveyed were teased by their families, compared to 34 percent of overweight boys. Note that this is not teasing as in harassment but rather simple statements made tongue in cheek: "Are you sure you should eat that?" or "Whoa there! That milk shake will go straight to your thighs!"[24]

A Crash Course on Cellulite

In addition to giving your daughters a healthy view of dieting and nutrition, you might also want to give them some fast facts on cellulite. They'll hear many myths regarding the cause and prevention of cellulite. This issue was brought to my attention recently when following a link someone had sent me to a posting on TMZ.com (popular celebrity gossip site). I was horrified to discover that they had snapped a photo of an eighteen-year-old celebrity from the backside as she peered through a storefront window and had created a viewer poll about the photo. This celebrity is known for having obtained the culture's ideal of the perfect body. Well, nearly perfect. The only problem was that the picture showed, gasp, CELLULITE on the back of this starlet's thighs. Oh my! Within twenty-four hours, more than eighty-seven thousand people had participated in the poll, the majority voting that it was a "bad picture" versus "a case of cellulite." More than two hundred readers commented; and while many expressed outrage over the site's crossing a line and sending a message to our girls that further narrows the definition of beauty, others will give you a taste of what our daughters are up against. Here is a sampling of comments by readers:

No. No. She is too young for cottage cheese legs. She must wait until she is a least 30 and has had kids!!!!!!!!

So young !?! So FAT !!!

Can you say hail damage?

YUCK!!

Let's hear it for TMZ: inspiring eating disorders worldwide.

PLEASE!!! This is hardly cellulite! This is not even fat! And we wonder why Nicole Richie, Mary-Kate, and thousands of young girls are anorexic! Come on TMZ!

it is natural, and i am glad to know that there are still some natural women in hollywood. her legs are thin, or are they only considered thin if she is anorexic or surgically altered? cellulite or not, she is beautiful. this report reminds me that our society is doomed . . .

Is it any wonder that so many young women and young girls suffer from eating disorders? TMZ just added yet another "nail in the coffin" of self-esteem for women all over the world.[25]

Fast Facts Regarding Cellulite

- Cellulite begins to appear in girls around the age of fourteen and increases as they mature and the subcutaneous skin layer thins and redistributes. Cellulite often forms in postnatal women and those who take birth control pills because the waste system can't get rid of the enormous flow of estrogen in the body.[26]
- Cellulite is far more common in women than in men (around 85 percent of women have it) because of the nature of the connective tissue under a woman's skin, which determines the way subcutaneous fat would be stored. Specialists assert that cellulite formation begins

in adolescence when the body begins to produce the female hormone estrogen. This hormone enlarges the cells under the skin, and the lymph fluids that pass through these cells begin to accumulate. The fat cells are compressed and harden, resulting in the appearance of what we call cellulite.[27]

- Cellulite is not linked to being overweight. Skinny people have cellulite. Young people have cellulite. Celebrities have cellulite, and super models have cellulite.[28]

- Common cellulite myths: Drinking more water will reduce cellulite; Exercise will prevent cellulite; A healthy diet will prevent cellulite.[29]

> Skinny people have cellulite. Young people have cellulite. Celebrities have cellulite, and super models have cellulite.

Let's stop making *cellulite* such a dirty word and educate our daughters to the fact that it's part of the uniqueness of being a woman. And while you're at it, if you have sons, make sure they are aware of how common it is among women and have not bought the culture's lie regarding the narrow definition of beauty. I, for one, am deeply concerned about the airbrushed images that our young men have been inundated with and left to believe this is, in fact, attainable. We can't minimize the influence this narrow-minded culture has had on our sons as well.

CHAPTER THREE

Buyer Beware:
Exposing the Media Lies

C hances are you remember the rumblings in the news about the American Psychological Association and their ground-breaking discovery that the proliferation of sexualized images of girls and young women in advertising, merchandising, and media is harmful to girls' self-image and healthy development.[1] When I heard it on the news, I stared at my TV in total disbelief and mumbled, "Nah! Ya think?" The study took aim at everything from sexually salacious ads to the tarted-up Bratz dolls popular with young girls. Every forum of media was fair game, including video games, song lyrics, magazines, and the round-the-clock bombard-ment of sexual images found on television and the Internet.

Sexualization was defined by the task force as occurring when a person's value comes only from her/his sexual appeal or behavior, to the exclusion of other characteristics, and when a person is sexually objectified, i.e., made into a thing for another's sexual use. While the overall finding of the study may not come as a surprise, it should serve as a wake-up call for parents who have somehow rationalized that it's a battle not worth fighting. Take a look at some of the fall-out the study confirmed:

- Cognitive and Emotional Consequences: Sexualization and objectification undermine a person's confidence in and comfort with her own body, leading to emotional and self-image problems such as shame and anxiety.
- Mental and Physical Health: Research links sexualization with three of the most common mental health problems diagnosed in girls and women—eating disorders, low self-esteem, and depression or depressed mood.
- Sexual Development: Research suggests that the sexualization of girls has negative consequences on girls' ability to develop a healthy sexual self-image.[2]

Parents: Problem or Solution?

> Parents can play a major role in contributing to the sexualization of their daughters, or they can play a protective and educative role.

According to the task force report, parents can play a major role in contributing to the sexualization of their daughters, or they can play a protective and educative role. The study acknowledges that parents may actually contribute to the sexualization of their daughters in a number of ways. One way is to convey the message that maintaining an attractive physical appearance is the most important goal for girls. As abhorrent as it is, we have all heard rumblings about parents who even go so far as to pay for plastic surgery for their daughters, whether it's a nose job at sixteen or a boob job for graduation. It certainly leaves their daughters clear on where mom and dad stand on the importance of vanity.

Before we look at ways to protect our daughters from sexualizing messages from the media, we must first examine ourselves to see if perhaps we have propagated this damaging message. If outer appearance is important to you and out of balance, chances are you have passed the same mind-set onto your daughter. Hopefully, after reading this section you will have a better grasp on why God tells us that we are "fearfully and wonderfully made" and further wants us to "know that full well" (Ps. 139:14). It may even be necessary to go to your daughter and apologize for the part you may have played in emphasizing outer appearance to an unhealthy degree. I have certainly had to own up to this in the past with my own daughter.

Next we need to put our daughters on a media diet. While it would be impossible to shield them from every damaging influence, we can certainly draw a line in the sand when it comes to the worst offenders. Below, you will find a list of the worst offenders and tips on how to limit your daughters' consumption and exposure to the damaging lies they generate.

Fashion Magazines

In the book *Teenage Girls: Exploring Issues Adolescent Girls Face and Strategies to Help Them*, author Ginny Olson states that

Early adolescent girls are especially vulnerable to media images. They're constantly searching for information to guide them as to how they should look and behave in this new world. As concrete thinkers, they haven't yet developed the necessary skills for discerning the different messages the media is sending. It's not until they reach about middle adolescence that they begin to develop the ability to scrutinize media messages and evaluate the themes with a certain level of skepticism. By the time they reach 17 or 18, they've had enough experience with the media to be able to assess and reject the messages.[3]

Study after study is proving that fashion magazines have a direct correlation on behavior among young women. One study of 548 middle school and high school girls found that 59 percent reported they were displeased with their bodies. When the researchers went a step further and investigated the impact of women's fashion magazines on the girls, they found that 69 percent of the girls said that the way the models looked in the magazines impacted their ideal of how the perfect female body should look.[4]

> Sixty-nine percent of the girls said that the way the models looked in the magazines impacted their ideal of how the perfect female body should look.

A University of Minnesota study found that teenage girls who frequently read magazine articles about dieting were more likely five years later to practice extreme weight-loss measures than girls who never read such articles. The study further found that "girls in middle school who read dieting articles were twice as likely five years later to try to lose weight by fasting or smoking cigarettes, compared to girls who never read such articles. They were three times more likely to use measures such as vomiting or taking laxatives." Coauthor of the study, Patricia van den Berg offers this advice to parents: "It possibly would be helpful to teen girls if their mothers didn't have those types of magazines around."[5]

One has to wonder if the primary agenda of the fashion magazines is to create a level of dissatisfaction among their female readers regarding their overall body image in an effort to keep them running back for more and more advice on how to achieve this impossible beauty ideal. As they absorb this message that their worth and value stem from their outer appearance and their chief aim is to please the opposite sex, parents are left to sweep up the mess in the years to come. As a longtime opponent of fashion magazines and their message of objectification to our young women, I would love to see parents put them in the same dangerous category as drugs and alcohol. It's time to ban this harmful filth from our homes and begin the detox process if we or our daughters have bought into the lie.

Music

When I was growing up, the word *slut* was whispered under one's breath and used sparingly. In fact, I can only recall a handful of girls who earned the label in my large high school of more than two thousand students. If you were labeled a "slut," your reputation was sealed. You were the brunt of boys' locker room talk and an instant outcast among the girls. The only thing missing was the scarlet letter.

Today, the word is commonplace in every teen's vocabulary. In the process of researching for my book, *Logged On and Tuned Out*, I saw the word posted everywhere by girls and guys alike on the social networking pages. Here are some actual examples:

Hannah, you look like such a slut in this picture!

Call me when you get home, slut!

Hey slut, when are you back from vacation?

Maybe I'm just turning into an old fuddy-duddy, but for the life of me, I don't get it. Since when did it become a compliment to be called a slut? Good girls are called sluts. Bad girls are called sluts. Church girls are called sluts. If your daughter is in high school or older, chances are, she's been called a slut. And unless you step in and do something about it, she will probably just smile and shrug it off as a term of endearment.

> Good girls are called sluts. Bad girls are called sluts. Church girls are called sluts.

Seriously, it's hard for me even to type the word; it was so taboo in my generation. Which begs the question: How did such a word become so acceptable? Hmmm, let's see. Could it be the hip-hop/rap culture that cranks out song after song depicting women as "hoes" whose lifelong aspiration is to serve their "pimps"? I did a little research on the Billboard Top 100 songs over the past twenty years, and my findings for the most part directly link the onset of the hip-hop/rap genre with the verbal degradation of young women.

The rating system for music began in 1985 which labeled certain songs as "explicit." From 1987 to 1994, there were, based on my own observation, on average, one to three songs in the Top 100 with explicit ratings each year. From 1995 to 2000, there were, on average, four to eleven songs in the Top 100 with explicit ratings each year. From 2001 to 2004, it jumped to twenty-three to thirty-two songs in the Top 100 with explicit ratings. Approximately, one in three songs in the Top 100 are explicit. Of the thirty-two songs with an "explicit" rating in 2004, twenty-seven were in the hip-hop/rap genre.6 These are the songs being played over and over again on the pop radio stations, MP3 players, and at school dances. And we wonder why it's become acceptable and even in vogue to be called a "slut."

While many argue that this is an acceptable form of artistic expression among those in the African-American community, I beg to differ. The impact has been felt across all racial lines. African-American or not, what self-respecting woman would condone such a verbal assault? And the abuse is not limited just to name-calling. Hip-hop music videos have inspired dance moves that are being played out at middle and high school dances, drill team, cheer performances, and the like. My daughter was involved in cheerleading (both competitive and high school level), and I logged six years of watching dance performances inspired by the hip-hop genre. It's a sad state of affairs to say the least. Whether it's a pack of pint-size grade school girls booty dancing at a cheer competition or a drill team grinding at a high school pep rally, I felt a lump rise up in my throat every time.

I know I'm not alone in my frustration. Over the years I have heard from mothers whose talented girls spend years in dance or cheer classes only to have to give up their dream at the high school level when they see what is required to make the team. I have heard from some girls who have walked off the team in an effort to take a stand, only to be teased and taunted for doing so. I even heard from a vice principal at one high school several years ago, who said that their drill team coach attempted to turn in a receipt for red boas from Frederick's of Hollywood for reimbursement. Ah, our tax dollars at use.

I have heard from other parents who have logged complaints only to have their daughters punished in return. I know this can happen because I was one of two parents who complained about a sultry dance move when my daughter was on a competitive cheer team in her freshman year. The owner of the gym agreed to change the move, but when the other girls asked why it was being changed, the coach jokingly said to blame it on my daughter and another girl on the team. Yes, these things do happen.

If we are to counter the culture's lie that our daughters are nothing more than objects, it's time to ban our children from buying and listening to songs that objectify women and take a stand when schools, and other cheer/dance organizations, allow the imitation of these objectifying dance moves. While I realize that it's nearly impossible to monitor each and every song our children listen to or upload to their MP3 players, you might consider banning songs that fall into the rap/hip-hop genre or requiring preapproval before they load them. If a song comes onto the radio and lyrics clearly objectify women, turn it into a teachable moment before you change the station. Ephesians 5:3–4 says, "But among you there must not be even a hint of sexual immorality, or of any kind of impurity, or of greed, because these are improper for God's holy people. Nor should there be obscenity, foolish talk or coarse joking, which are out of place, but rather thanksgiving." I feel pretty certain that words like *slut, hoe,* and *hooker* would fall into that category.

TV, Movies, and the Internet

Another media influence that can fall on the worst offender list for objectifying and sexualizing our girls is television, movies, and the Internet. As they get older, it's nearly impossible to monitor every TV show and movie they may watch, not to mention every Web site they might visit, but we would go a long way to ban movies and block shows that are known for being sexually provocative or explicit. I highly suggest that parents block channels like MTV, VH1, and other like-minded cable channels that are known for their constant objectification of women. Additionally, sit in and listen to the shows your kids are watching to ensure they are appropriate, and take advantage of sites like www.pluggedinmagazine.com and www.screenit.com to review movies before allowing your children to see them. Also, the Parents Television Council (www.parentstv.org) rates the most popular shows among kids and compiles a "best and worst shows" list based on the content. They also have a fabulous feature where you can select a popular show and read the corresponding review.

When it comes to objectionable Web sites, I highly recommend that parents install Web filters and monitoring software to add as many layers of protection as possible. It will be impossible to protect them 100 percent of the time; and as they get older, they can access these channels/shows at friends' houses. This is why it is of utmost importance that parents take advantage of critical moments and point out the media's objectification of women as well as discuss the fallout that can result.

Fashion

Whether it's popular clothing retailer Abercrombie and Fitch's screen-print tees with messages like "Who needs brains when you have these" or the 1.6 million dollars spent on thong underwear by girls aged seven to twelve, clearly we have a problem.[7] Victoria's Secret now has a line aimed at tween, teen, and college girls. It used to be that you didn't set foot into Victoria's Secret until you had a ring on your finger. My first exposure to the store was at my lingerie shower! Nowadays girls as young as middle school are stopping in to pick up a birthday present for their best friend. When I was a teen girl, we were begging our moms for one of those adorable Lanz flannel nightgowns and couldn't wait to show it off at the next sleepover. Mercy, what happened?

And if I hear one more person spin this skin-baring fashion phenomenon as "girl power" and proof that girls are more confident of their bodies, I think I'll throw up. I don't care if these girls have six-pack abs or ten pounds of flab hanging over the waistband of their jeans, they need to cover up their midriffs. Clearly I have reached my limit of uninvited hoochie-sightings.

Just recently, I was at the grocery store and caught a glimpse of a girl squatted down in front of the freezer case, apparently reading the label on a product. Coming out the backside of her pants was the T-strap of her thong underwear. I'm not even sure why she bothered to wear pants since every passerby was subjected to what was underneath. What particularly struck me was the clear lack of concern or awareness that she had as others passed by. For heaven's sake, didn't she feel the cool breeze on her backside? Or was she desensitized to the fact that exposing your undergarments (or crack) just might be considered inappropriate to a large segment of the population?

Now I don't know if I was just in a grumpy mood that day or fed up in general with yet another display of TMT (too much thong), but I approached this young lady, tapped her on the shoulder, and kindly whispered, "I don't know if you know it, but your underwear is showing." I said it with a sincere motherly, trying-to-spare-you-some-embarrassment sort of expression and tone. I must have pulled if off because she immediately stood, adjusted her britches, and actually mumbled a "thank you" under her breath. If it sparked even a vague awareness that showing your undergarments in public places might not be appropriate or appreciated by other passersby, then mission accomplished.

> As parents we must help our daughters realize that their clothing is like a label.

As parents we must help our daughters realize that their clothing is like a label. When they wear skin-baring fashions, it often sends a message to others about their character. Surveys show that it is not screaming, "Girl Power" or "self-confident," but rather, "I'm available," or, "Bring it on." The APA study that I cited previously had this to say:

If girls purchase (or ask their parents to purchase) products and clothes designed to make them look physically appealing and sexy, and if they style their identities after the sexy celebrities who populate their cultural landscape, they are, in effect, sexualizing themselves. Girls also sexualize themselves when they think of themselves in objectified terms. Psychological researchers have identified self-objectification as a key process whereby girls learn to think of and treat their own bodies as objects of others' desires. In self-objectification, girls internalize an observer's perspective on their physical selves and learn to treat themselves as objects to be looked at and evaluated for their appearance.[8]

Let me break that powerful statement down for you. When we (parents) allow our daughters to dress in a revealing manner, we play a part in sexualizing and objectifying them. Not to mention, many girls are not yet able to make a connection between what they wear and the reaction it may generate among the opposite sex. The APA study found that "girls are experiencing teen pressures at younger and younger ages. However, they are not able to deal with these issues because their cognitive development is out of sync with their social, emotional and sexual development. Let girls be girls."

In Shaunti Feldhahn's fabulous book *For Young Women Only*, she cited the results of a survey where guys were asked questions pertaining to the way girls dress. The study found that when girls dress in such a way as to call attention to their bodies, 85 percent of guys said that they would have a temptation to picture her naked (either then or later). The survey further confirmed that the majority of guys thought she was dressing that way because she wanted them to picture her that way. Her survey of girls found that in reality only less than 4 percent of girls dress in a revealing fashion in an attempt to get guys to fantasize about them.[9]

It is up to us to have this necessary conversation (over and over again) with our daughters and remind them that clothing sends a strong message; and it may, in fact, be a message that misrepresents who they really are. When it comes to sporting the perfect outfit, we need to let our daughters know that there is nothing wrong with dressing fashionably as long as it meets God's standard of dress—"modestly, with decency, and propriety" (1 Tim. 2:9).

Airbrushed Images

Time, wrote John Milton, is "the subtle thief of youth." Perhaps there is no more painful reminder of that truth than a torturous afternoon spent trying to find the perfect swimsuit to flatter a post-forty shape. Did I say flatter? I meant HIDE! See, there I go, exposing my own susceptibility to the media's lie that forty is the new thirty.

> Time, wrote John Milton, is "the subtle thief of youth."

Give me a break. While I don't watch (or endorse) *Desperate Housewives*, I've seen enough pictures of these women to know that they have all had Photoshop makeovers, ahem, not to mention, a few other costly makeovers as well. With slews of images like that, is it any wonder women of all ages are resorting to Botox injections, plastic surgery, and break-the-bank skin care regimes that promise to take ten years off their lives?

Recently the popular Dove Campaign for Real Beauty sought to expose the general public to a more realistic picture of aging when they released pictures in an ad campaign of older women in the equivalent of their undergarments. They were untouched images that exposed the reality of the natural aging process. They were healthy-sized women with curves, dimples, cellulite, and age spots.

While there was controversy over the ads being too racy to be in magazines, part of me was glad to see at least an attempt (though radical) to expose the media's antiaging obsession.

Sometimes the challenge seems insurmountable when it's everywhere we look. *Redbook* magazine was criticized for putting thirty-nine-year-old, country music star, Faith Hill on the July 2007 cover and photo-shopping the picture to lengthen her neck, slim her arms and thighs, trim her waist, and airbrush away her wrinkles.[10] *Redbook*, for heaven's sake! My grandmother used to subscribe to *Redbook* because it wasn't considered a fashion magazine. In *The Beauty Myth: How Images of Beauty are Used against Women*, author Naomi Wolf said, "Magazines, consciously or half-consciously, must project the attitude that looking one's age is bad because $650 million of their ad revenue comes from people who would go out of business if visible age looked good."[11]

How do we even begin to tackle this topic with our daughters and give them a more realistic picture of the natural aging process? How can we convince them that "gray hair is a crown of splendor" (Prov. 16:31) when many of us, myself included, are rushing to our hairdressers and paying them to cover it up, one gray hair at a time? Ouch! I for one am not feeling so led to give up my highlights, occasional manicures, and magical eye cream, so it's important to find a balance. Are you at peace, for the most part, with the aging process, or are you kicking and screaming about every gray hair and facial wrinkle?

I recently stumbled upon some interesting information regarding the aging process. If you're young, read it and weep. If you're old and your kids are kind enough to remind you on a daily basis, read it and weep and then torment your kids with the information! According to an article on CNN.com, there are six stages of life: infancy, childhood, adolescence, young adulthood, middle adulthood, and senior adulthood.

The description of young adulthood is what caught me by surprise. Here is what it says: "A person reaches physical maturity and stops growing around age 18. As early as age 20, people may notice the beginning signs of aging; fine wrinkles, thinning skin, loss of firmness in hands and neck, graying hair, hair loss and thinning nails. At age 30, the human body's major organs begin to decline."[12]

The other day when my daughter and son made a comment about some straggly gray hairs on my head, I smiled this really evil smile and said, "Well darlin's, your turn is a-comin', and it may be sooner than you think." I then seized the opportunity to inform them that their bodies may show signs of aging in their twenties and their organs will begin shutting down around thirty. OK, so maybe "shutting down" is a bit harsh, but I was trying to make a point. Apparently, they missed the point because my son replied, "Well duh. Everyone knows thirty is old." Oh my. Looks like I have my work cut out for me.

We need to make sure our daughters realize that the images they are seeing in the media of models and celebrities who appear to have found the fountain of youth are not real. Most have been prepped for the photo session by hair and makeup artists, Botox, plastic surgery, and even after all that, will likely be airbrushed beyond recognition. We need to set a positive example for our daughters and make friends with the aging process. That doesn't mean we have to let our hair go gray and wear it in a tight bun atop our heads and fill our closets with holiday sweaters and Naturalizer footwear. I for one enjoy dressing fashionably, getting my hair highlighted, walking to keep my legs toned, and using a bit of self-tanning lotion to cover some of my spider veins.

> We need to set a positive example for our daughters and make friends with the aging process.

There is nothing wrong with beautifying the temple as long as it's done in good taste and is not your primary focus. If our daughters are constantly subjected to our grumblings as we journey through the aging process, it will leave them with the impression that life is somehow less appealing in the latter years. Seriously, who wants to go back to their teens and twenties?! Let's quit this nonsense of being shocked and surprised when our bodies begin to show some wear and tear. Some (if not many) of the most beautiful women I know are over fifty and put the polished and airbrushed models and celebs to shame. The over-forty cast of *Desperate Housewives* couldn't hold a candle to these women when it comes to true beauty. Will you be one of them?

CHAPTER FOUR

Redefining Beauty

Mothers, did you know that only 2 percent of women would describe themselves as beautiful?[1] Are you in that small sampling? Is your daughter in that small sampling? After discussing in depth the lies both we and our daughters have been told regarding the narrow definition of beauty, we are left with the task of redefining beauty. Only then can we pass along a healthy definition to our daughters.

What exactly is beauty? The Dove Campaign asked women and found that:

> Only 2 percent of women would describe themselves as beautiful.

- Seventy-seven percent strongly agree that beauty can be achieved through attitude, spirit, and other attributes that have nothing to do with physical appearance.
- Eighty-nine percent strongly agree that a woman can be beautiful at any age.
- Eighty-five percent state that every woman has something about her that is beautiful.[2]

Interestingly, the study found that two-thirds of women strongly agree that physical attractiveness is about how one looks, whereas beauty includes much more of who a person is. Women rate happiness, confidence, dignity, and humor as powerful components of beauty, along with the more traditional attributes of physical appearance, body weight and shape, and even a sense of style.[3]

Now, stop for a minute and think about it. When you hear (or say) the phrase, "She is beautiful," is it made in reference to what is on the outside or the inside? I find it sad that popular culture and the mass media have hijacked the authentic definition of beauty. Beauty is defined by God and God alone. He sets the standard for beauty and gives us clues throughout Scripture as to what defines a beautiful woman. Unfortunately, the secular definition of beauty given by women in the Dove survey failed to recognize the key component that determines a woman's happiness, confidence, dignity, and humor. That key component, of course, is faith. Just as the Proverbs 31 passage concludes, "Charm is deceptive, and beauty is fleeting; but a woman who fears the LORD is to be praised" (Prov. 31:30). Faith in a loving and forgiving God will be the root of any and all manifestations of beauty. Physical beauty will fade over time, but true beauty (virtue) is timeless.

Damage Control

As parents, that's where we come in. Only by pointing out the lies of culture and continually reminding our daughters of God's definition of beauty (virtue) will we stand a chance of protecting our daughters from the culture's inevitable brainwashing. We must be faithful in reminding them that beauty is not defined by a number on the scale, a premanufactured clothing size, an hourglass shape, washboard abs, slender thighs, big boobs, a J-Lo butt, pouty Angelina Jolie lips, a pair of designer low-rise jeans, a cleavage-baring top, a new sassy haircut, a clear complexion, an antiwrinkle cream, or a surgical procedure. While some of the above may garner catcalls from men, they don't impress God in the least.

If we are to engage successfully in the worthy conversation, "You are more than the sum of your parts" with our daughters, we must first do a self-check and make sure we believe it ourselves. For those of us who have been thoroughly brainwashed by the culture over the years, this will be a difficult challenge. And, I dare say, that would likely be the majority of women reading this book! In fact, while in the course of writing this book, I conducted an informal survey of adult women and asked, "Are you satisfied with your body/appearance?" Only a handful of the women answered yes to that question.

While I realize that many women struggle to achieve a healthy weight range and, therefore, may not be satisfied, I was even more concerned with the answers that followed on the next question. "If your weight fluctuates beyond your desired weight range, does it

> **O**nly by pointing out the lies of culture and continually reminding our daughters of God's definition of beauty (virtue) will we stand a chance of protecting our daughters from the culture's inevitable brainwashing.

affect your overall happiness?" Even among the women who had previously answered that they were currently satisfied with their body/appearance, most admitted that should their weight fluctuate, like the others who answered the survey, it would impact their overall contentment/happiness. While I hope that this book will help you better engage in the necessary and ongoing conversation with your daughters regarding body image and appearance, I pray that the truths presented will aid you in breaking free from the culture's lies.

In a world that beckons our daughters to grow up far too fast, it's never too soon to begin the conversation with our daughters regarding true beauty in the eyes of God. Below I have compiled some key Scripture verses related to appearance and beauty and an example of how you might explain the meaning behind each verse to your daughter. Some are verses I have referenced in preceding chapters, but they bear repeating! Wouldn't it be nice if our girls grew up with the following verses tucked away in their hearts?

Beauty by the Book

Psalm 139:14	I praise you because I am fearfully and wonderfully made; your works are wonderful, I know that full well.

What it means: You are created in the image of God, and God doesn't make junk! Like a snowflake, every person is unique. No two are the same. God sees you as a masterpiece; and when you look in the mirror, He wants you to "know that full well." Try this beauty tip: Every morning when you look in the mirror, say Psalm 139:14 and smile. You might even tape the verse on your mirror as a reminder!

| *1 Samuel 16:7* | But the LORD said to Samuel, "Do not consider his appearance or his height, for I have rejected him. The LORD does not look at the things man looks at. Man looks at the outward appearance, but the LORD looks at the heart." |

What it means: The world focuses on what people look like on the outside. God focuses on what people look like on the inside. Do you put more time and effort into being pretty on the outside or the inside? As you get older, you will meet Christian girls who spend more time trying to find the perfect outfit, get the perfect tan, find the perfect lip gloss, and have the perfect body. While there's nothing wrong with wanting to look pretty, we need to make sure it's in balance. God would rather see us work on becoming drop-dead gorgeous on the inside. You know, the kind of girl who talks to Him on a regular basis (prayer) and reads her Bible.

| *Proverbs 31:30* | Charm is deceptive, and beauty is fleeting; but a woman who fears the LORD is to be praised. |

What it means: Beauty fades with age, so if you are more concerned with your outer appearance, you will be unhappy when the wrinkles come and the number on the scale goes up. In fact, did you know that your body may show the beginning signs of aging as early as age twenty? That is why God wants us to "fear" Him. That doesn't mean to be afraid of Him but rather to be in awe of Him and all that He has done. Let me put it to you this way. If you stand two girls next to each other and one is Miss Teen USA whose beauty is limited to physical beauty, and the other young lady is a more average-looking girl who loves the Lord more than anything, she is the more beautiful girl in the eyes of God.

1 Peter 3:3–4	Your beauty should not come from outward adornment, such as braided hair and the wearing of gold jewelry and fine clothes. Instead, it should be that of your inner self, the unfading beauty of a gentle and quiet spirit, which is of great worth in God's sight.

What it means: This does not mean it's wrong to braid your hair or wear nice clothes and jewelry. The verse was written to warn women not to follow the customs of some of the Egyptian women who, during that time period, spent hours and hours working on their hair, makeup, and finding the perfect outfit. God would rather see women work on becoming beautiful on the inside—the kind of beauty that lasts forever.

1 Timothy 4:8 NLT	Physical exercise has some value, but spiritual exercise is much more important, for it promises a reward in both this life and the next.

What it means: Exercising and staying in shape is a good thing, but God expects us to stay in shape spiritually by reading our Bibles, praying, and going to church on a regular basis. In other words, there will be plenty of people who put their time and effort into staying in shape but who are out of shape spiritually. If they don't know Jesus Christ, their perfect bodies won't get them through the gates of heaven.

If Your Daughter Is Five Years or Less

I would be willing to bet that most compliments paid to infants and toddlers are in regard to appearance. Of course, this is understandable considering we can't really highlight an infant's sparkling personality or good deeds accomplished. Chances are we heard, "What a beautiful baby," on numerous occasions when our daughters were just infants. And chances are, we have said it countless times to others. While our infants are unable to absorb the message, it won't be long before they do. My daughter, now eighteen, was often complimented as a baby for her blonde curls, blue eyes, fair skin, and teeny-tiny frame. She hardly looked old enough to walk when she took her first steps, and many claimed she looked like a little porcelain china doll. And trust me, by the age of two, she had taken note of each and every compliment.

I recall a day when she was just 2½ years old and we were walking by a shop window. She caught her reflection and said, "Oooohhhh, pwiddy gull." I laughed at the time, noting her confidence and wondering if it would bleed over into her teen years when she needed it most.

The appearance-based compliments (from others and myself) continued through her toddler years. Until an occasion when she was four years old, I didn't realize there might be a downside to the praises. It was picture day at her preschool and I had dressed her up in a beautiful dress with a matching hair ribbon that held back her sweeping long blonde curls. As she was walking into the door of the classroom that morning, her teacher said, "Paige, you look so pretty!" Paige's response without even missing a beat was, "I know. Everyone tells me that."

Yikes! Of course, this was long before I was writing about the dangers of misdefined worth, not to mention I was hardly qualified since I was clearly part of the problem. From that day forward, I tried to emphasize her character qualities and de-emphasize her physical beauty. If she grew dependent on the compliments, what would become of her self-esteem when she entered the gawky, adolescent phase? You remember it, don't you? Pimples, bad hair days, and a body that often seemed out of control—truth be told, many of us are still in recovery from those days!

We must be careful to find a healthy balance when it comes to complimenting our child's appearance, especially in the early years. On the one hand, our girls naturally *want* to be told they are pretty.

If we don't tell them, it could leave them craving male attention in the years to come. On the other hand, we don't want to go overboard and send a message that worth is based on what they look like. This, in turn, could set them up for disappointment when the compliments diminish over the years.

If Your Daughter Is Six to Eleven Years

As your daughter moves through grade school, she will begin to absorb the culture's message regarding beauty. Whether she is being influenced primarily by the media or her friends, one thing is for certain: she is hearing a buzz about what constitutes beauty in the world's eyes. It will be especially important in these years to have open communication with your daughter regarding these messages. Take advantage of teachable moments, whether they are ads you come across or a comment made by a friend. Remind her of 1 Samuel 16:17 and how God looks at the heart while the world looks at appearance. Continue to remind her of this passage as she moves through grade school. If she struggles with weight, emphasize a healthy diet and exercise and make sure you are practicing it yourself. Rather than nag her about eating too many sweets or snacks, try to reduce the temptation by minimizing them in your home. Lead by example. Whatever you do, never shame her about weight, even jokingly.

If your daughter seems to be overly attentive in these years to appearance and body image issues, you might want to look closely at her immediate circle to see where the influence is coming from. Is it a friend? Is she exposed to messages in the media that she is

> We must be careful to find a healthy balance when it comes to complimenting our child's appearance, especially in the early years.

too young to process? (For example, is she allowed to watch PG-13 movies, watch shows on TV or listen to music that supports a narrow and unrealistic definition of beauty?) Could you or your husband be focusing too much on appearance and sending her the wrong message? If you see warning signs, do what you can to reverse the damage, even if it means seeing a counselor or nutritionist. Many eating disorders take root in these years and, if not addressed, will only get worse.

Again, emphasize virtue and character qualities over appearance. This doesn't mean you go overboard and tell her appearance doesn't matter. The message should always be temple maintenance: healthy weight range, good eating habits, exercise, positive grooming habits. Because girls are developing earlier, your daughter will be exposed to many shapes and sizes during these years. It's important that you don't make comments about other girls (or your daughter) in these years that could leave them feeling inferior or worried about their own development process. As they move into the latter years of grammar school, begin necessary conversations with them about the process their body (and their friends' bodies) will go through as they move from girlhood to womanhood.

If Your Daughter Is Twelve Years or Older

When I surveyed adult Christian women, one of the questions I asked them was: "What sort of message did you receive from your mom and/or dad regarding weight/body image when you were growing up?" Many women shared that even today they could still remember exact phrases and the sting they felt over comments made by their parents during their middle and high school years.

"Are you sure you want seconds?"

"Have you checked the calorie count in that cookie?"

"You might want to lay off the _____."

"You're never going to get a husband if you keep eating like that."

Comments such as the ones above, made even in jest, will have an impact on our daughters. Even if your daughter needs to lose weight, it's best if the pediatrician breaks the news rather than her hearing it in the form of constant nagging by a parent. And for the record, if the pediatrician isn't worried, you shouldn't be either. Again, a better approach would be to emphasize nutrition and exercise and lead by example. Practice it; don't preach it.

For most of our daughters, the change in body shape will be most drastic in the span of years from twelve to eighteen. Most girls will have their womanly shape by the time they graduate high school. Many girls are caught off guard in these years when their bodies transition (almost overnight, it seems) from girlhood to womanhood. We must make sure they know that this is normal and part of God's design to prepare them someday to bear children. Never assume that they will naturally absorb that truth by osmosis! One adult married woman (age twenty-six) in the survey I mentioned above (who was in the handful of women who were content with their body shape and size) admitted that she was desperately afraid to have children for fear of gaining weight or changing her shape. Did her mother not warn her of this and speak of it in positive terms?

> **A**gain, a better approach would be to emphasize nutrition and exercise and lead by example. Practice it; don't preach it.

Having had an eating disorder that began in my high school years, I can speak firsthand of the struggle I had accepting that my adult figure would not remain in the 105 to 110 pound range. I'm not sure why I settled on this magical range of numbers as the barometer to my happiness, but it haunted me well into my early thirties. Once I was finished nursing my last child, I immediately began the same drastic measures I had taken in high school and college (starvation and fasting) to maintain a weight range that was not realistic for someone who had birthed three children and moved into her thirties. Finally, with the help of counseling and spiritual growth, I came to realize the extent of my brainwashing—a brainwashing that, mind you, began in my high school years. Today I have adjusted my attitude regarding what constitutes an acceptable weight range but still find myself lapsing back into the old lies from time to time.

One thing I have made an effort to do with my own daughter is to educate her to the reality of her weight and shape changing over the years. I don't want her to fall into the same trap that I did and mistakenly assume that she has reached her lifelong ideal weight (amazingly, the same weight I was at her age). While I have gained weight over the years, I am still in a healthy weight range so I point that out to her. I pray that as she witnesses my confidence, she will have a healthier attitude in the years to come. Even if you are not currently within a healthy weight range and are in the process of losing weight, you can still model a healthy attitude regarding weight and nutrition.

If your daughter is in the twelve to eighteen age range, make sure your comments related to appearance, weight, and body shape of your daughter (and others) are scarce. If you are preoccupied with these things, chances are, your daughter will be as well. Allow your daughter to hear you compliment women who are truly worthy of being labeled beautiful—those who are virtuous. Limit your daughter's exposure to the key offenders I mentioned in chapter 3; and when she is exposed to lies, take advantage of teachable moments. Most importantly, keep the conversation going over the years and remind her often, "You are not the sum of your parts."

Always a Work in Progress

Recently, I went to the doctor for a sinus infection, and the nurse said the words most every woman dreads before ushering me into a room. "Step on the scale, please." I've mentioned previously that in an effort to improve my attitude regarding body image, I put my scale away several years ago. Overall, it has done wonders in adjusting my attitude. Until now, that is. I felt too crummy to argue with the nurse, so robotically, I slipped off my shoes and stepped on the scale. I stood there as motionless as possible as she fiddled with the metal sliders and continued to move one further and further to the right until it landed on a number. I felt my heart begin to beat faster and faster. *Dag-nabbit. Was that a primal scream going off in my head?* Immediately, another number came rushing to my mind. You know the one I'm talking about: that stupid magical range of numbers that had defined my worth for so many years. I wish I could tell you that I immediately recognized the enemy's scheme and quickly readjusted my attitude by changing those negative tapes. Not so. Here's a glimpse of the tape that was playing in my head as I stepped off that scale: "Oh my gosh. Are you kidding me? Can that number be right?"

> Allow your daughter to hear you compliment women who are truly worthy of being labeled beautiful—those who are virtuous.

The tapes were briefly interrupted when the doctor entered the room and I was forced to focus on the real reason I was there—the other sickness in my head. But the tapes picked right back up again when I drove away, en route to get my prescriptions filled:

"OK, it's 2:00 p.m., and I've had breakfast and lunch, so that has to allow for at least two to three pounds. And my clothes, they have to weigh around two pounds. Add another pound for this cute but very heavy Brighton necklace. And all that congestion in my head—that has to be another couple of pounds, right?" (Wow, losing weight has never been so easy!)

At this point, something snapped and I realized the absurdity of the tapes running through my head. I gave the devil a stern talking-to in my car and thanked God out loud for seeing me as "fearfully and wonderfully made" (Ps. 139:14). I asked Him to help me in the ongoing pursuit to define my worth according to His standard of beauty rather than the world's narrow, not to mention unrealistic, standard.

Since that visit to the doctor's office, God has convicted my heart with yet another truth regarding the endless pursuit women face to be beautiful. Truly the quest to meet the world's standard of beauty is vain. Every thought that consumes my heart, every moment that my focus is deterred off Him and onto myself is nothing more than vanity. For the sake of our daughters, we must put this into the proper perspective and change our way of thinking when it comes to beauty. Maybe there's something to be said of the mirrorless days of the past where scales could only be found at county fairs and in doctor's offices and full-length mirrors had not made their way into homes. What would these God-fearing sisters of the past think of the never-ending focus our culture today places on physical beauty? I'm betting they might remind us of Ecclesiastes 12:8: "Vanity of vanities, saith the preacher; all is vanity" (KJV).

CONVERSATION 2

Don't Be in Such a Hurry to Grow Up

CHAPTER FIVE

Girlhood Interrupted

Just recently I was going through some old photographs and stumbled upon a heartwarming picture of my daughter and four of her friends at the tender age of nine. They were standing side by side and proudly posing, each one cradling her respective American Girl doll. I remembered taking the picture, their innocent smiles reflective of what being a "tween" girl is all about. I recall wondering, at the time, how much longer they would be content with dressing up their dolls and throwing them pretend birthday parties.

A couple of months after taking that photo, one of the same girls in the picture came over to spend the night and left her doll behind at home. Instead, she brought over a newly purchased CD. The mock birthday parties they used to stage with their dolls were replaced on this evening with a late-night concert, starring of course, my daughter and her friend. With the boom box blaring at top volume and their karaoke mics in hand, they were belting out the chorus of a new song, "Hit Me Baby One More Time," by an up-and-coming artist, Britney Spears. I wasn't familiar with this artist at the time, but she looked to be a mere child herself, posing innocently on the front of the CD cover with her hands in a prayer-like stance.

As I watched my daughter and her friend sing into their mics like little pop stars, it hit me at that moment that a battle was looming on the distant horizon—a battle, mind you, that would pit a concerned mom against a culture bent on robbing her daughter of her girlhood. How ironic that less than a decade later the pop star on that CD cover would become the poster child for all that can go wrong when you grow up at warp speed.

That day I only saw my own little girl and her friend standing on the banks and dipping their big toe in the water. The current was slow moving; and, though they appeared somewhat curious about what lay beyond, their feet were still firmly planted on the bank. Two years later, at the age of twelve, she would make the dreaded request to put her dolls away. Up until that point her dolls were a permanent fixture in her room, as much a part of the decor as the lime green velvet curtains and the fuzzy beanbag chair in the corner.

"Are you sure?" I asked, hopeful she would change her mind. "What if one of your friends comes over and wants to bring her doll?"

Without hesitation, she confidently declared, "Mom, we're twelve now. That's not going to happen."

I don't know what stung my heart more: the signal that the doll phase was over and out or the reminder that she was, in fact, twelve and one year shy of officially being a teen. And so I began the difficult task of neatly packing away her dolls, doll clothes, and doll furniture in sturdy, plastic storage bins—sensing at the time that it signaled the close of one chapter and the beginning of another. I tried desperately to stifle my tears as I shoved the bins onto the top shelf in her closet. I reasoned that their new home was far superior to the hot, stuffy attic and much more convenient should my daughter change her mind and decide to release her dolls from their plastic prison. In my heart I knew the top shelf would likely remain their permanent home.

Today my daughter is eighteen and in her first year of college. Packing her dolls away was minor in comparison to packing her belongings and moving her into a dorm more than five hundred miles from home. Where did the time go? It seems like she hardly noticed the transition from little girl to tween, tween to teen, and now teen to young woman. Oh, but I did. And I did my best to make sure she relished each and every season. At eighteen she stands at the crossroads of girlhood and womanhood and dances back and forth between the two. On the one hand, she is a typical teen who is never far from her cell phone and checks her Facebook page daily. But this same girl will occasionally wear loose braids and plan her weekend around a Hannah Montana marathon on the Disney Channel.

The culture has beckoned her to grow up far too fast, but for the most part, she managed to plug her ears and hang on by a thread to her girlhood. Proudly, my daughter was ten going on ten, sixteen going on sixteen, and now, eighteen going on eighteen. A good majority of girls her age left the shallow banks of girlhood far too soon and were swept along by the fast-moving currents of the culture. And unfortunately, many have bumps and bruises to show for the journey.

> **A** good majority of girls her age left the shallow banks of girlhood far too soon and were swept along by the fast-moving currents of the culture.

Many of you reading this find yourself where I was when I was packing away the dolls. One day your daughter is very much a little girl, and the next day she is showing signs of restlessness. Others of you perhaps are breathing a huge sigh of relief that you're not there yet. Enjoy the days you have, and don't rush your little girl to grow up. Fight for every moment of her girlhood, and don't allow the culture to get its foot in the door. Perhaps others are reading this, and your daughters are being swept away in the current. You desperately want to throw them a lifeline, but you're not even certain they would reach for it. You may be thinking, *Too little, too late.* No! Don't give up that easy. In fact, let me give you this hope: You are the great and mighty gatekeeper when it comes to providing your daughter with a much-needed umbrella of protection. In other words, you have the power to say "yes," "no," or "wait" when these influences come knocking. If you haven't set parameters in advance, it won't be easy, but it's not impossible.

If I had to pinpoint one common denominator that is commonly shared among girls who grow up too fast, it would be this: a set of parents or a parent who, for whatever reasons, stood by on the shoreline and allowed their daughter to wander in too deep. Many, I dare say, even cheered their girls on as if there was some sort of prize at the finish line. What type of parent would allow this to happen? Below, I will describe four styles of parenting that create the perfect storm for raising a daughter who can be on the fast track to growing up. You may want to dog-ear this page and refer back to these parenting styles when reading the remaining two chapters in Conversation 2 dealing with peer group influence and issues pertaining to boys and dating.

Dangerous Parenting Styles

"Buddy buddy" Parents. There is nothing wrong with being your child's friend as long as you are the parent first. These

"buddy buddy" parents are more focused on being their child's friend than their parent and will often attempt to avoid conflict in an effort to stay in favor with their child. Buddy buddy parents are lax on boundaries and prone to giving into requests made by their child. A root cause of buddy-buddy parenting is low self-esteem. Being viewed as "cool" by their child and their child's friends can be a boost to esteem. Ironically, the child is rarely sincere about the friendship and plays along to manipulate the results. Additionally, the parent's true motive in seeking to be best buds is not really done for the goal of prioritizing the child; rather it's about the parents' need for approval.

"Buddy buddy" Parents. There is nothing wrong with being your child's friend as long as you are the parent first.

Even if you do not embrace this parenting style, you need to be aware that there are many parents who do. While working on this chapter, I was tipped off by a concerned parent to some disturbing photos on Facebook of a party that took place at the home of a student from my children's high school. Fortunately my children were not in attendance at this party where alcohol was flowing freely from a keg in the garage and the kitchen counter was littered with Keystone beer cans.

I was thinking, *Where in the world are the parents?* when suddenly I found my answer: a picture of good ol' dad in the kitchen posing with some of the girls, each of them with a beer in hand. And another picture of dad's girlfriend posing in between two high school guys who appear to be holding her up. By the looks of the picture, I suspect she's filled up her cup one too many times at the keg she and good ol' dad probably purchased. I even found another picture of dad's girlfriend "booty-dancing" with one of the girls in the kitchen. Aren't they "cool"? They're so "cool," I took a screen shot of the pictures and saved them to my desktop. I don't know this couple, but I couldn't help but wonder if the parents of the other kids at the party (or the police for that matter) would think they're cool for supplying alcohol to minors. Parents like this disgust me. Do they not realize that they are partially to blame if one person leaves that party intoxicated and an accident occurs?

"Too Busy to Care" Parents. These are typically the parents who are running themselves ragged in their jobs or activities and left with little time to be engaged when it comes to parenting their child. Parenting is hard work and takes tremendous amounts of time and energy to stay engaged in what is going on in their child's life. Drawing up boundaries, maintaining the boundaries, and addressing issues when the boundary lines are crossed take time. If time is short, these parents put aside parenting and only address critical issues as they arise, often reacting only after the damage has been done.

"Too Tuned Out to Notice" Parents. These are typically the parents whose temperaments lend themselves to a more laid-back parenting style. While being laid back can be a positive quality in parenting, it can also be a detriment if it results in few boundaries and little, if any, boundary enforcement. Again, because parenting requires round-the-clock diligence and an ability to stay engaged in the issues impacting our children, "too tuned out to notice" parents often fail to see what's going on around them. These parents are the most likely to extend too much benefit-of-the-doubt to their kids and say things like, "Kids will be kids," or, "What I don't know won't hurt me." Unfortunately, it may hurt the child.

"Living through My Kid to Feel Better about Myself" Parents. Oh boy, if you haven't seen these parents in action, head to the nearest ball field/cheer gym/booster club meeting for a sighting. The root of this type of parenting is usually low self-esteem and a need to please/impress others. "Look at my child! He/she is popular/

athletic/smart/attractive" you-fill-in-the-blank; and therefore, that makes the parent feel *important*. Another end result of this type of parenting is an unhealthy concentration on "image maintenance." These are typically the parents who make sure their child looks good and performs well at all times since they typically see their children as reflections of themselves unless, of course, the children fail and then we have a problem. If children succeed, parents feel like they succeed. And if children fail, parents take it personally and blame the child/coach/teacher or whoever is nearby to point blame. Therefore, failure is not an option.

So, there you have it—four styles of parenting that can lead to our daughters growing up too fast. Truth be told, many of us (myself included) may lapse into one or more of the parenting styles above from time to time. Only by looking to God for strength and wisdom when it comes to parenting our children will we find the proper balance needed.

Managing the Milestones

A few years ago while on a visit to see my mother, we went through a box of keepsakes she had gathered throughout my younger years. We stumbled upon a hilarious, laugh-out-loud letter I had written to her in my fifth-grade year. The general theme behind the two pages of clumsy cursive boiled down to this: "Mom, can I please, please get a bra?" The desperate plea then followed with a list of every girl in the fifth grade who had already gotten a bra and stated, "I am the only one who doesn't have one!" Ever hear that line before?

The letter worked and I got my bra. I can still picture in my mind the visit to the department store and the excitement of picking one out. It had to have been a size AAA and probably stayed puckered in the cups for a good two years before I finally filled it out. I in no way *needed* one at the time, but that didn't seem to matter. My friends had triggered the bra alarm; and, therefore, it was time to get one.

Another alarm would again sound in sixth grade, and I would begin that joyous and never-ending journey of shaving my already-hairless legs. I went through box after box of Band-Aids from nicking my ankles and shins, but I proudly wore them like badges of honor. Besides, I almost wanted someone to ask, *"Hey, what happened to your leg?"* so I could proudly respond, *"Oh, it's no big deal. I just cut myself shaving."* It was an unspoken litmus test of all things cool. In sixth grade there were shavers, and there were nonshavers. God help you if you were a nonshaver, especially if your legs looked like a boy's legs.

And so it continued through the years. The alarm would sound, and off we'd rush to get our first spiral perm, pair of designer jeans, Hang Ten velour shorts, bikini swimsuit, haircut with Farrah Fawcett wings, *Seventeen* magazine subscription, boyfriend, or job. Every milestone signaled that we were leaving behind the "little girl" years and were well on our way to growing up. And just as is true with our own daughters, our time line for "growing up" didn't always match up with our parents' preferred time line. It helps to reflect back on those years and try to remember what it was like to be our daughter's age. Often we snap into the mom mode and forget how important some of these issues were to us when we were that age. It's perfectly normal for our daughters to want to experience the same milestones other girls their age are experiencing in a timely manner. Their greatest fear is to be the last one to fall in line or, even worse, not be in line at all.

While we don't want to jump the gun and say "yes" too soon, we also don't want to go overboard in saying "no" or "wait" to milestones that are reasonable. For example, I had a friend in grammar school who felt uncomfortable swimming and wearing shorts in the summer because her legs were hairy. (Gasp! A nonshaver.) She needed to shave, but mom and dad had imposed a rule that she couldn't shave until seventh grade. That's the rule they had in place for her older sister, and by gum, the same rule would apply to her. Never mind that her legs were beginning to look like Chewbacca's on *Star Wars* by the end of sixth grade, . . . or so the boys told her.

> **W**hile we don't want to jump the gun and say "yes" too soon, we also don't want to go overboard in saying "no" or "wait" to milestones that are reasonable.

Finding a reasonable balance is important. What's right for my daughter at a particular age may not be right for your daughter at that same age and vice versa. Below are some general guidelines regarding some of the most common battles we will encounter in our daughters' growing-up journey. (Note: I will cover issues related to peer group and boys in the following two chapters.) The experience of having logged eighteen years' worth of battles with my own daughter, as well as my outreach to preteen and teen girls through ministry, has afforded me the ability to keep a pulse on the issues that often catch mom off guard.

Who among us is really prepared when our sweet little angels are begging to go to Build-A-Bear one day and get a bra the next? Or a cell phone? Or a Facebook page? Or heaven forbid, thong underwear? And trust me, the age they start asking keeps getting younger and younger. What will you say? Mothers, these are common milestones faced by non-Christian and Christian girls . . . yes, even good, little, sheltered Christian girls. In presenting these common issues, my goal is to give you as much background as possible before your little one comes calling and leaves you gasping with your hand to your heart.

A Disclaimer

Before we go over this list, let me make several disclaimers. First, allow me to issue a gentle caution to mothers with daughters younger than high school. Some of what you read below may leave you frustrated and wondering why "a good Christian mother" trying to raise "a good Christian daughter" wouldn't just draw a firm line in the sand on every one of these issues and issue a firm NO! Easier said than done. What I have discovered in parenting my own "good Christian daughter," as well as ministering to many across the nation, is this: like it or not, many, if not most, of our "good Christian girls" are drowning in a sea of cultural pressures that cannot even begin to compare to what we were up against at their same age.

That said, parenting is far more complicated than issuing a standard no to their every request. There is a fine balance in drawing firm boundaries in some areas while, at the same time, being willing to compromise in other areas. Girls who hear *no* over and over again often rebel out of sheer exasperation with the rules and boundaries. We can all think of examples of darling Christian kids who, once out of the eye of their overprotective Christian parents, go crazy berserk with their first taste of freedom.

I know this is hard to believe when your daughter is still naturally compliant and doodling "I ♥ Jesus" on the front of her spiral notebook at school. Girls like that don't grow up and ask for thong underwear, right? Wrong! I guess what I'm asking is that you withhold judgment. Trust me, I was you! Overall, my daughter has fared well in the growing-up journey and has caused me few, comparatively speaking, problems along the way. She has emerged at eighteen with her girlhood and her innocence still intact. However, she is not perfect, nor am I. And yes, I gave in on some issues that I had at one point boldly stated, "My daughter will never _____." I'm sure this is where the "never say never" phrase probably originated—with Christian mothers who, like me, had to eat those very words for breakfast, lunch, and dinner.

You would think I would have learned my lesson when my kids were toddlers after stating (in my first pregnancy) a few bold declarations such as: "My child will *never* have a pacifier!" (Result: All three used a "passie" until the age of three.) Or how about, "My child will *never* sleep in our bed!" (Result: My daughter spent many a night in the first two years of her life in our bed. Sleep deprivation will make you recant most anything.) Or even a more recent, "My children will *never* attend public school!" (Result: I put all three in public school for high school.) Now I'm the one who goes around chanting, "Never say never."

This leads me to my second disclaimer: I am not an expert. Even though I may state a personal opinion of how I handled a particular issue in my home with my daughter, it may not be the best solution for you and your daughter. Sometimes, as Christians, we can have a tendency to see black and white on issues that God never intended to be black and white. So please keep that in mind as you read on.

The Latest Media Gadgets. Cell phones, MP3 players, laptops, DVD players, and the like will attempt to wiggle their way into your daughter's life soon enough. Limit her from spending too much time on things that distract her from more positive influences such as face-to-face relationships, board games, outdoor play, creative play, reading, learning to play an instrument, and time spent with family. Don't overindulge her by getting the latest gadget as soon as it comes out. It's healthy to wait and it breeds a greater appreciation.

When you do say yes, take it slow. For example, when you get her a cell phone, don't load it up with unlimited text messaging, a ton of minutes, and the ability to send and receive pictures and videos. You will have to decide what age is appropriate for your child, but remember, you are the parent, and you can always change your mind if you discover after the fact, that they are not ready.

Fashion. It's disturbing enough to see teen girls (or young women in general) emulate the scantily clad celebrities and their skin-baring fashions, but it's incomprehensible that many children's and junior's departments now offer pint-size hooker-wear. Expect to hear, "But Mom, everyone wears this!"

Draw a firm line in the sand on this one. Your daughter is not an object for the male viewing pleasure—not now or ever. If Conversation 1 didn't convince you of that, I don't know what will. Set the rules on the front end: no exposed cleavage, super-tight T-shirts, microminis, exposed midriffs, exposed bra straps, shorts with hoochie messages written across the backside, and whatever else you feel a need to add to the list. There have been occasions where I have sent my own daughter back upstairs to change and other times where she has walked in the door in "borrowed" clothing from a friend that didn't meet my approval. Mistakes will be made along the way. Always be faithful in reminding her about the why behind the rule (plenty of ammo in Conversation 1!).

Media (TV, Movies, Music). Studies show that kids who are exposed to sexually explicit song lyrics, as well as television shows such as those on MTV, are more likely to have early sex. Pay attention to song lyrics, movie ratings, television shows, Internet activity, and other media influences that have adult themes and draw appropriate boundaries.

Be particular about what you allow into your home; it is your right and responsibility to protect the innocence of your children. Case in point: After reviewing the lyrics on the Britney Spears CD my daughter and her friend were listening to at the tender age of ten, I refused to buy it for my own daughter. I used it instead as a teachable moment to explain that the meaning behind the lyrics portrayed girls as objects.

If they own a MP3 player, check their song libraries from time to time and make sure you don't see songs with explicit ratings. Don't give them carte blanche privileges to watch whatever they want in the way of TV shows and movies. Different families have different rules when it comes to what they will and will not allow their children to watch in the way of television and movies. Make sure your daughter is aware of your standards for times when she is away from home. This can be a difficult or awkward situation for her if her friend's family has more liberal standards, so help your daughter come up with a plan or something tactful to say when faced with the situation.

> **B**e particular about what you allow into your home; it is your right and responsibility to protect the innocence of your children.

Online Communication. I have written an entire book for parents on this topic (*Logged On and Tuned Out*) and addressed it in my magabooks for tween girls (*Between*) and teen girls (*TeenVirtue*). I am a big proponent of both safety filters and monitoring software. The latter tracks key strokes made and e-mails the reports to your in-box. With one in five children having been solicited for sex online, failure to track what our kids are doing online seems irresponsible to me. The software I use sends me a report of Web sites visited and actual transcripts of IM conversations.[1] My kids know it's on our home computers, so there's a level of built-in accountability.

IMing. The age keeps getting younger and younger for IMing. Hold off as long as possible. When you do say *yes*, get a screen name of your own and participate with your child. Make sure the computer is in a central location and spot-check your child's buddy list from time to time. Again, monitoring software is a must as it allows you to spot-check actual transcripts of IM conversations. Set reasonable time limits. Also, educate your child about cyber-bullying, as well as the dangers of clicking on links, which could lead to inappropriate sites or a virus. Again, as with the cell phone, start slowly and ease her into it by adding privileges along the way.

MySpace/Facebook. Your child should not be on these sites before she reaches the minimum age. Doing so requires her to lie—and trust me, many (Christian) kids are doing just that. Only you can decide if your child is ready at the minimum age, but I implore you to be involved. You have every right to require your daughter's log-in and password information and spot-check her page. In fact, you have a responsibility. That is exactly what I do with my younger son (age fifteen). I quit logging onto his older two sibling's accounts right around their junior year in high school. They had proven themselves trustworthy, not to mention they were months shy of being on their own.

Lingerie (Bras/Padded Bras/Thongs). Let's start with bras. Use your own discretion based on your daughter's development, but I caution you against buying her a "padded bralette" that could send a wrong message. There's a balance in finding a bra that covers her sufficiently yet doesn't add a whole cup size in the process. My daughter wore a sports bra for many of her young years, and it did the trick. Just don't wait so long that it puts your daughter in an uncomfortable situation, especially if she is showing signs of development.

Now onto the fun topic of thongs. Honestly, I hate that our girls even know about them. I understand that many God-fearing Christian girls (high school and older—please don't tell me they're younger than high school!) wear them for practical reasons such as a disdain for panty lines. Not liking panty lines myself, I can relate to their logic on some level. Regardless, here are some facts you need to know before saying yes. I recently shared them with my own daughter, and I could tell they made an impact.

An increasing number of reports link thong underwear to recurrent urinary tract and vaginal infections. One ob-gyn said, "The thong is like a little subway car. (Eww!) The bacteria goes from the rectum to the vagina and to the bladder."[2] Another ob-gyn offered this advice: "Underwear is supposed to provide a soft barrier between you and irritants such as your clothes. So as tempted as you are to wear them every day, I wouldn't encourage it. Save them for special occasions."[3] Straight from the doctor's mouth, so you don't have to be the bad guy if you want to say no. And if you decide to say yes, it's still a good idea to pass along the health concerns to your daughter and encourage her to wear thongs sparingly.

Tattoos and Piercings (Other Than Ears). Fortunately, this trend reached its peak during the Britney-era and has died down since. However, allow me to indulge you with some facts regarding both, should your daughter express even a vague interest. According to the Mayo Clinic, "A tattoo or piercing may take only a few minutes or hours to acquire, but invest plenty of thought and research before getting one. If you take steps to protect yourself from possible risks, what seems like a cool idea now is less likely to turn into a source of regret later."[4] The risks include blood-borne diseases, skin disorders, skin infections, and allergic reactions. Should your daughter be among the many who someday wish to remove their tattoos, she needs to know that "tattoos are meant to be permanent, so their complete removal is difficult. Several removal techniques exist, but regardless of the method used, scarring and skin color variations are likely to remain."[5]

When it comes to piercings (other than the ears), the risks include blood-borne diseases, allergic reactions, oral complications, skin infections, scars, and keloids.[6] My personal philosophy on both tattoos and piercings is that there is a high likelihood of regret years down the road. Given their permanent nature, why risk it? Not to mention, surveys show that many guys do, in fact, judge a girl based on tattoos and piercings. (I also covered this issue in *TeenVirtue: Real Issues, Real Life . . . A Teen Girl's Survival Guide.*) I don't personally see the purpose; however, I have younger friends who are precious Christians and have chosen one or the other (or both). My daughter has not expressed an interest; however, I broached the topic just prior to dropping her off at college. Just to make sure there were no surprises, I made clear that a decision to pierce or mark her body needs to wait until she is out of college and off our payroll.

When it comes to the temptation to grow up too fast, I am reminded of the description of Susan in C. S. Lewis's classic Narnia book, *The Last Battle*:

> "She's interested in nothing nowadays except nylons and lipstick and invitations. She always was a jolly sight too keen on being grown-up."

> "Grown-up, indeed," said the Lady Polly. "I wish she would grow up. She wasted all her school time wanting to be the age she is now, and she'll waste all the rest of her life trying to stay that age. Her whole idea is to race on to the silliest time of one's life as quick as she can and then stop there as long as she can."[7]

Lewis seems to echo the sentiments of Ecclesiastes 3:1, "There is a time for everything, and a season for every activity under heaven." Girlhood will last only for a brief season and, once gone, can never be revisited. Why rush this precious time? It's up to us to help our daughters enjoy the ages they are now rather than the ages they may wish to be.

> **"There is a time for everything, and a season for every activity under heaven."**

CHAPTER SIX

The Friendship Factor

In my first magabook for teen girls, *TeenVirtue*, I wrote an article called, "Help! My Best Friend Has Gone Crazy Wild!" Having served for many years in girls' ministry, I knew that the title depicted a common challenge faced by many Christian girls. As parents, we cannot underestimate how the friendship factor can play a part in rushing our girls to grow up too fast. We see many well-meaning Christian parents lose the grip they have on their daughters when they loosen their grip on their daughter's peer group. If you have a daughter in middle school or older, you've probably witnessed the dramatic shift that takes place when it comes to the importance of friendships. During these years our daughters begin to prioritize peer approval over parent approval. And if the shift caught you off guard as it did me, be encouraged that studies confirm that it's not personal.

Ginny Olson notes in her book *Teenage Girls: Exploring Issues Adolescent Girls Face and Strategies to Help Them* that it's important for mothers to realize that "although their daughters may seem to be distancing themselves, they aren't seeking total autonomy." She goes on to share the results of research by Dr. Terri Apter of the University of Cambridge, who has studied mothers and daughters for more than twenty years. In her research she found that daughters aren't seeking a "divorce" from their mothers; rather, they're seeking to redefine the relationship in the midst of their changing world. Apter states, "The 'task' of adolescence is not to sever the closeness, but to alter it."[1]

Until this point our daughters may have given little thought to choosing their friends. In other words, most of their early friendships just happened, whether they were mom-initiated or resulted from being in the same homeroom. As our daughters mature and become more capable of exercising independent thought, we begin to see them take a more active approach to choosing their friends. They will naturally seek out those they most identify with, or for some girls, those they *desire to* identify with. They may even experiment with several different peer groups until they find a good match. At this point, they may choose to part ways with the friends they had in the earlier years or, in some cases, the friends we hand-picked for them. This can be especially difficult if some of their old friends just so happen to be "family friends."

Parents need to keep a close eye on their daughter's friendships in these years and, if need be, step in if they see warning signs that indicate their child is associating with a high-risk peer group. Parents are often hesitant to step in and take an active role when it comes to influencing their child's peer group. Unfortunately, this is where many girls wander off course, especially if their parents have adopted one of the four parenting styles discussed in the previous chapter.

For those of you with younger daughters, I know it's hard to imagine that some of your daughter's precious friends could someday be on the banned friend list. However, if you think back to your own younger years, I'm sure you can recall perfectly sweet and precious girls who went hog wild in middle or high school. Maybe you were that girl leading your friends to the nearest mud bath.

I've often joked that as a mother I've done my best to protect both my daughter and my sons from the girls like me (at their age)! And trust me when I say that I had plenty of "church girls" in my peer group who were all too happy to follow my lead! The remainder of this chapter will address why it's important to stay tuned-in to our daughter's peer group, as well as how to go about staying involved.

You Are Who You Hang Out With!

Associate yourself with men of good quality if you esteem your own reputation. It is better to be alone than in bad company.

—GEORGE WASHINGTON

The type of friends your daughter chooses or gravitates toward can speak volumes about her developing identity. It's hard to say whether "identity determines peer group" or "peer group determines identity," but the point is really moot. Either way your daughter has willingly chosen to conform to a peer group; and, depending on the nature of that peer group, it can have a positive or negative outcome on her behavior. Until middle school most of the friendship concerns we have with our daughter are likely related to the standard issues of girl politics: cliques, mean girls, rejection, hurt feelings, etc. By middle school we begin to see clues that indicate which girls are on the fast track. Pay attention to those clues because they can serve as a warning sign of things to come.

The type of friends your daughter chooses or gravitates toward can speak volumes about her developing identity.

Technology can provide a window into the hearts and souls of not only our children but also their friends. By monitoring my children's activity on the social networking sites, I have been able to pinpoint "toxic peer groups" in each of my children's respective grades and, thus, caution them to steer clear at all costs. You can count on at least one idiot at every party who will take pictures and upload them to their Facebook or MySpace page, usually within twenty-four hours. If your daughter is associating with a high risk peer group, it is only a matter of time before she will be "tagged" in a picture for all the world to see. Hopefully she's not the girl throwing up in the toilet, mooning the camera on a dare, or playing beer pong with a group of friends.

The National Longitudinal Study of Adolescent Health surveyed more than ninety thousand adolescents on many health-related issues and evaluated peer influence (specifically related to teen pregnancy). The study found that, on average, a girl's risk of pregnancy decreased one percentage point for every 1 percent increase in low-risk friends versus high-risk friends she has in her peer group. The study also noted that a couple of high-risk female friends in a girl's crowd are not that dangerous and do not necessarily hasten first intercourse or increase the risk of pregnancy.[2] The key, rather, seems to rest on having a majority of low-risk friends.

On the other hand, having high-risk male friends and older friends of both sexes increases girls' risk of negative behaviors. And while having low-risk male friends is protective, high-risk male friends may place girls at heightened risk for pregnancy.[3] Again, this study focused specifically on peer group and the influence of pregnancy; however, I think their conclusions can be applied across the board to other dangerous behaviors. Just this year I was made aware of a situation involving a beautiful young lady in high school (sophomore) who was accustomed to getting a good deal of attention from older boys. Unfortunately her mother found this flattering and was known to brag about the many boys, some even college aged, bidding for her daughter's attention. Months later this precious girl withdrew from school for a drug problem and was headed to rehab. I was told the parents were devastated and had been completely caught off guard upon their discovery of the problem. Suffice it to say, this girl was yet another sad statistic of girls who are allowed (and sometimes *encouraged*) to grow up far too fast. Why any parent would willingly expose their daughter (purposely or by default of neglect) to situations that are well beyond their years is beyond me.

Having high-risk male friends and older friends of both sexes increases girls' risk of negative behaviors.

While I am on the topic of allowing our girls to hang out with older boys who are on the fast track, let me also issue a warning about the social networking sites. In my book *Logged On and Tuned Out*, I cover in depth the dangers of allowing children to participate on these sites before they reach the minimum age (high school) and without parental supervision, such as monitoring software. But perhaps the best warning is the following chilling comment I received on my blog from a reader:

> My daughters are 11 and 13 and we don't allow them on these sites yet. One week ago tonight, their little 13-year-old friend (from their discipleship group at church)

committed suicide. She was a beautiful girl, smart and spunky—an excellent athlete—deeply loved with lots of friends and a family that loved her dearly. But she wanted to grow up quickly. Just this year she attended her first middle school dance. There were 750 people at her funeral this week . . . tons of middle-schoolers from church, from school, from her soccer team. No one can even begin to understand why. But her mom made one plea to the kids at the funeral—and that was to stay off MySpace. She shared that her daughter was on MySpace and that last weekend she got on her daughter's account (after her death). She said people (men) from all over the world were contacting her—men old enough for her (the mom) to date. It's a very sad story, and I would guess there are more like it around the country. Moms . . . parents . . . stay involved in your kids lives—pray for them and protect them.

Mothers, we cannot underestimate the dangers of exposing our daughters to a high-risk peer group, whether it's online or in person. As a parent, you have every right to have a vote when it comes to your daughter's choice in friends. If your daughter runs with a crowd that is eager to grow up, she will behave in like manner. Encourage your daughter to spend time with girls who are comfortable acting their age.

Helping Your Daughter Choose a Positive Peer Group

Benjamin Franklin once said, "He who lies down with the dogs, shall rise up with fleas." If you've ever had to treat a flea-infested dog, I think you'll agree that it's far better to take preventive measures on the front end than to tackle the problem after the fact. When it comes to choosing a positive peer group, one distinction we have made in our home is the difference between "weekday friends" and "weekend friends." A "weekday friend" might be someone my child meets at school or an after-school activity. The friendship is primarily built during school hours or during the time spent in a common activity. Any time spent after school or on weekends would be at our home in a monitored environment. A "weekend friend" might be someone who has similar beliefs and values as my child. I would not hesitate to have this child over on the weekends or allow my child to spend time with the friend away from our house.

Obviously, the "weekend friend" list is much shorter list than the "weekday friend" list. Having taught our children this distinction, we have a baseline for helping them choose a positive peer group that is parent approved. For example, if my child expresses a desire to get together with a "weekday friend" from school and it is a friend we don't know, we have the condition that the friend come to our house until we can get a better gauge on the situation. The friend may or may not transition into a "weekend friend." In some situations, our children had friends they strictly saw at our home because we did not have an adequate comfort level in allowing our children to spend time at the friend's house.

The National Longitudinal Study of Adolescent Health study concluded that parents have a good reason to get to know their children's friends as well as the parents of their children's friends. Researchers found that, with regard to a girl's risk of intercourse, her friends' closeness to their parents is equally as important as the girl's relationship with her own parents because girls whose friends have poor relationships with their parents are at greatest risk for earlier sexual activity.[4]

Based on these findings, here are some ways the researchers suggested parents can remain vigilant about the influence of their child's peer group:

* Look beyond your child's best friend to his or her close circle and wider peer group to understand the full range of peer influence.
* Pay attention to the composition of your teen's immediate circle of friends.
* Relax about the effect of one or two risky female friends on your daughter. On average it is not harmful for "good" girls to have a few high-risk female friends. And your daughter's friendship may be good for those high-risk friends by helping reduce their risk. (**Note:** I would caution parents to use discernment; and if the risky female friends display a pattern of encouraging your daughter to engage in high-risk behaviors, I would consider issuing a ban.)
* Focus more on your teen's positive friends. These are the peers who are making a difference. Helping young people sustain positive relationships with good role models is protective.
* Pay close attention to high-risk boys and significantly older friends of both sexes in your daughter's circle of friends. Their influence can be negative.
* Learn about the relationships your child's friends have with their parents. By steering your children to friends who are close to their own parents, you can help reduce risk.[5]

Do whatever it takes to make it possible for your daughters to spend time with girls who share the same values and would make good "weekend friends." My daughter moved from a small private school to a large public school when she began high school and had a difficult transition when it came to finding friends who shared the same values. She spent many weekends at home during those first couple of years; and while it certainly spared her from many temptations, it was difficult for her all the same. During those years I did whatever

I could to help her maintain contact with some of her friends from her old private school (on one side of town) as well as our youth group (the other side of town) who had proven to be good, solid "weekend friends" over the years. Eventually, she was able to drive and connect with them on her own. Even though these girls will scatter to different colleges now, they will remain on her treasured list of life-long friends. It was worth the effort. It was worth the added time. It was worth being picky. Not one of these girls was in a hurry to grow up and it shows.

> **D**o whatever it takes to make it possible for your daughters to spend time with girls who share the same values and would make good "weekend friends."

Forbidden Friendships

It may be necessary in some cases to ban your daughter completely from high-risk associations for a season (or sometimes permanently) when boundary lines are crossed or trust is breached. Both of my older children experienced a major stand-at-the-crossroads, life-defining situation in their high school years. Keith and I have always prayed that if (when) our children stray from the path of God, they will be caught in their sin as early as possible. Simply put, we asked God to sound the sin alarm to "Repent! Turn back!" Should our children respond by hitting the snooze button, we wanted them caught so we could intervene in an effort to: (1) address the problem at its root cause, and (2) protect them from straying any further down the path before they develop a negative habit or pattern. In a nutshell we wanted them caught before they could hit the snooze button.

My son's wake-up call arrived in the summer prior to his junior year. My daughter's wake-up call arrived in her senior year and is still fairly fresh as I write this. Both situations had to do with lying about their whereabouts in order to attend parties where alcohol was present (and consumed). In both situations, they were caught (just as we had prayed) and, as a result, immediately placed on lockdown. In addition to seizing their cell phone, laptop, and car keys (with the exception of driving to school and work), we also banned them from associating with anyone else who had been involved in the situation until we could get a better grasp on the situation. We reasoned that these "friends" were not a good influence on our child; and our child was in turn not a good influence on them.

Because a breach of trust had occurred, the burden of responsibility was placed on our child to earn the trust back before privileges were reinstated. In both situations we identified certain friends who, because of a proven track record of distrust and a lack of repentance, were put on the banned friend list permanently unless they could prove otherwise. I know this sounds harsh, but given the power of peer influence, we have a responsibility to protect our children. Sometimes this means drawing boundaries that would aid in protecting them from *themselves*. This forced our son to have to find a new peer group halfway through high school, but God was good and provided a handful of solid Christian friends. Today he admits that our "friend ban" forced him to reevaluate his faith and pick a set of friends that shared his same faith and values at a critical time in his life. Had we not done so, I can only imagine how far off course he may have wandered. Our daughter's situation led her to conclude that some of the "friends" who attended the party are not worth the risk of associating with on any level other than casual acquaintance. She, too, views her experience of being caught as well as the "friend intervention" as much needed wake-up calls to rouse her from a spiritual slumber.

We have been fortunate that for the most part, our children have made overall good choices when it comes to their immediate peer group. The few bumps along the way served as tangible reminders of God's wisdom when it comes to choosing friends. Truly, "bad company corrupts good character" (1 Cor. 15:33). And we must accept that in spite of our time and attention teaching them this truth, sometimes our children will have to learn it the hard way.

How Well Do You Know Your Child's Peers?

1. Name your child's best friend.
2. Name your child's next closest five or six friends.
3. Do you know those friends' ages?
4. Name those friends' parents' first names.
5. Describe those friends' relationships with their parents.
6. Name as many young people as you can in your child's peer group (usually about fifty individuals).
7. Describe the social and behavioral characteristics of the leading (most popular) crowd at your child's school.
8. Describe the social and behavioral characteristics of your child's school.[6]

Bad company corrupts good character. (1 Cor. 15:33)

CHAPTER SEVEN

Boy, Oh Boys!

If there had been a Boy Crazy Club in grade school, I would have been the president. I can't recall the exact moment boys appeared on my radar, but I'm pretty certain I can trace it back to the "I like you" note that I passed Bill Anderson in my fourth-grade homeroom class. When he replied back in his fourth-grade boy-scribble admitting that he liked me too, I passed it around to all my best girlfriends who, in turn, responded by finding their own boy to pass a note to. It was as if our cooties inoculations had simultaneously worn off and a new truce had been called. These same annoying creatures that had at one time made our skin crawl now mysteriously made our hearts beat faster and our cheeks flush when they so much as glanced in our general direction or breathed our same air.

Maybe boys didn't make it on your radar as early as fourth grade, but I'm betting you still have memories of when it did. And as hard as it is to imagine, your daughter will chalk up plenty of her own memories when it comes to cooties, crushes, and all things boys. Yet in spite of the fact that this is a normal occurrence in the growing-up process, most mothers will be completely and totally caught off guard when it occurs, unsure of how to respond or react. Should girls be allowed to go out in middle school? IM, text, or talk on the phone? Go to the mall or the movies? Sit next to the boy they like on the field trip? What about when they hit high school? Is it really realistic that they could hang out in groups for the full four years? What does "Christian dating" look like? Is there even such a thing? Is old-fashioned courtship realistic? Seriously, where is the guide-book to delineate all the details?

As someone who has been in ministry to both girls and mothers through the years, I am happy to share some observations I have made along the way regarding this controversial subject. In addition, now that my own daughter has journeyed through the middle and high school years, I have some additional insight as well. Am I an expert? No! Goodness, I'm just like you—hanging on by my fingertips in this crazy ride called motherhood. There are many different attitudes regarding the topic of boy-girl relationships, especially when it comes to what is appropriate and acceptable for our Christian kids. Some of you reading this chapter will think my approach is too conservative. Others of you may think my approach is too liberal. The important thing is that you take the matter before the Lord and come up with a plan of your own that best suits your daughter's temperament. Proverbs 15:22 says, "Plans fail for lack of counsel, but with many advisers they succeed." Just view me as one of many advisers. You know your daughter best, and what has worked for my daughter may not work for your daughter. But this much I do know: Have a plan and, preferably, get it in place before the tough issues start coming down the pipe. Those who fail to have a plan will, by default, send the message to their daughters that the world's brand of dating is acceptable and those girls will mold their attitudes accordingly.

Young Love: Grammar School Romances

Oh, how I wish an older, wiser mother had taken me aside when I was laboring over the episodes of young love in my home and told me to take a chill pill. When I look back now in hindsight and think of all the hand-wringing I experienced over trying to decide if my son should be allowed to buy the girl he liked in fifth grade a stuffed animal for Valentine's Day or whether my daughter should be allowed to send the boy she likes a note from summer camp, I want to slap myself silly. Trust me when I say that you can overanalyze some topics, and this is one of them. When all was said and done, all three of my children experienced the thrill of "young love" at some basic level and had a few stuffed animals and love notes to show for it in the end. And shock of shocks, the world continued to rotate on its axis.

Proverbs 15:22 says, "Plans fail for lack of counsel, but with many advisers they succeed."

Middle School: The "Going Out" Experiment

I was pretty low-key when it came to the experimental phase of "going out." My mantra during those years was, "You can call it going out, but you're not going anywhere!" Of course, they were required to hang out in groups, and no couple time was allowed. Ever. With my two older children, their experimental going-out phase was fairly uneventful and, quite honestly, resulted in their clamming up and talking less with the other person once the relationship officially transitioned to the "going out" status. Another rule I had in place was that they not refer to the other person as their "girlfriend" or "boyfriend." That tends to elevate the relationship to the world's level of dating.

My younger son had a slightly different journey with his going-out experiences since IMing and texting had become more prevalent in middle school. Because kids feel more comfortable typing and texting things they wouldn't normally say to someone's face, it removed the natural barrier of awkwardness that was common when learning to communicate with the opposite sex. I encourage you to have some boundaries in place for communication with the opposite sex, regardless of whether you allow your child to "go out." I also recommend that you consider limiting or banning text messaging and possibly even taking the phone up at night. I did this for a time when I discovered that girls were texting my youngest son at all hours of the night in his eighth-grade year.

Also, I highly recommend that you not allow your daughter to participate in the social networking sites prior to high school. The minimum age on some sites is fourteen, but many middle schoolers are lying about their ages in order to participate in this forum. This is one area where kids are being allowed to grow up far too fast. As I've mentioned before, I recommend that you install monitoring software on the computer your child uses. There is much to be said for this built-in accountability, especially if they know you are receiving periodic reports of their activity.

Finally, if you find that your daughter's definition of going out models the world's brand of joined-at-the-hip dating, put a stop to it. This is yet another area where girls are growing up far too fast. Remember, you are the parent, and you have the right to change, adjust, or even abolish your rules along the way. If you allow this "experimental going out" in these years, the key is to keep it low-key and inconsequential.

High School: The Date or Not-to-Date Debate

If ever you need to be extra attentive to your daughter's level of interest in boys, it's during her high school years. Honestly, this is the season of life where her dating attitudes will be molded. If you have not begun to lay the groundwork for what you deem to be acceptable and unacceptable, she will get her cues from the culture at large. Having witnessed so many female casualties in my ministry to girls, I walked into my daughter's high school years loaded for bear and ready to fight for a better standard. Of course, I was up against the challenge of finding that tricky balance where you draw firm boundaries yet, at the same time, allow for a little breathing room so she doesn't grow exasperated and stage an all-out rebellion. Below are some rules we put in place on the front end of her high school experience and a brief explanation of the *why* behind each one:

Remember, you are the parent, and you have the right to change, adjust, or even abolish your rules along the way.

- I told my daughter that she would not be allowed to date or go out with a boy prior to her junior year, and at that point we would evaluate the situation (should there be a suitor) on a case-by-case basis. Why this rule? I cannot think of a single case in all my years of ministry to girls where a serious dating relationship during the early years of high school produced, overall, positive results. Maybe exceptions can be found, but I am not aware of a single one. Most girls are not emotionally, physically, or spiritually prepared to handle the responsibility and drama that comes with an exclusive dating relationship. Not to mention, you are playing Russian roulette with her purity when you allow the dating process to begin at such an early age. I have watched good Christian girls fall like flies in their high school years because they thought they were strong enough to have a serious boyfriend and follow Jesus at the same time. By drawing a firm line in the sand on the front end, my daughter knew it wasn't up for debate and, therefore, concentrated on hanging out with male friends, as well as building her female friendships.

• Once my daughter was allowed to date or go out with someone, she knew that part of the process was that her father would have a chat with the young man to make sure he was aware of our rules, curfews, and expectations in the relationship. In doing this, we knew that it would require our daughter to be more thoughtful and selective when it came to the character of the young man in question. In other words, many guys would cut and run upon hearing about this requirement. Good riddance, I say. If he truly cares about our daughter, he will stick around and rise to the level or our expectations. Interestingly, when I reminded my daughter of this requirement a few weeks into her first dating relationship, she did not give me any flak over it. In fact, a few days later, I asked her if she had mentioned to the young man that her father wished to speak with him, and she replied, "Yes, and he said he totally respects that." Good sign, I said. Good sign.

• While under our roof, an approved dating relationship will never be allowed to escalate to the "joined at the hip" status that is all too common in the high school years.

Other than the obvious fact that the more time a couple spends together one-on-one, the more likely they will eventually succumb to physical temptations, it also deters from quality time spent with family, friends, and, most importantly, God.

We emphasized to our daughter that she should consider only dating Christians. The truth is, you marry someone you date, so dating someone who is not a Christian is not worth the gamble. If he doesn't share the same values and beliefs, the relationship isn't worth pursuing. Period. End of sentence. Run fast and run far. Dating should never be a mission field. There's too much at stake to risk it. Oftentimes it backfires, and the Christian ends up relaxing her values in an effort to make the relationship work.

> **D**ating should never be a mission field.

Long before my daughter had her first official boyfriend, I told her to prepare and practice her speech detailing her physical boundaries and told her that it wasn't a matter of *if* she needed the speech but *when*. Most girls give into physical temptations for lack of a plan. It's too late to come up with a plan when the windows are fogging up in the backseat of a car and your boyfriend is whispering sweet nothings in your ear. The fact is, much of the sex teen girls are having is unwanted. In a study of 279 female adolescents published in *Archives of Pediatrics and Adolescent Medicine 2006*, nearly 41 percent of girls ages fourteen to seventeen reported having "unwanted sex" and claimed they did so because "they feared the partner would get angry if denied sex."[1] Furthermore, of a dozen possible topics in sex education, 84 percent of girls asked to hear more about this number one topic: how to say no to a boyfriend's requests for sex without losing the boyfriend.[2]

How did this new and revised definition of dating work out, you might wonder? My daughter did not experience a dating relationship until the second semester of her senior year of high school (just recently). I am ever so grateful for the delay in that it enabled her to gain some maturity along the way. By the time she began to date, she had witnessed the fallout many of her friends suffered from their own dating experiences and taken note of their heartaches. One added advantage I had in my corner that delayed the dating process was that my daughter was a late bloomer. While this was at times frustrating for her, I was counting my blessings that the boys were paying more attention to the girls who, let's just say, were looking more like young women than little girls. Of course, by her junior year, she had evened out with most of her friends, and the guys began to notice. I responded by gently suggesting that she revisit her nose-picking habit from her toddler years in a last-ditch effort to ward the boys off a bit longer.

If your daughter is showing signs of early development, just a heads-up that you could face a bigger challenge when it comes to keeping the boys at bay and your daughter disinterested. It is difficult to push the pause button in the rush to grow up when your daughter is already wearing your same bra size . . . or bigger. Girls who develop at an earlier age are often noticed by the older boys as well as treated the age they look rather than the age they are. As a mother, you will have to work overtime to minimize this effect. And certainly, don't encourage the attention. I have always been amazed at the mothers who brag about the male attention their daughters receive for being more developed. Or for that matter, who can forget the creepy statement made by Jessica Simpson's father, Joe Simpson, in defense of her less than wholesome fashion choices when he said, "If you put her in a T-shirt or you put her in a bustier, she's sexy in both. She's got double Ds! You can't cover those suckers up!"[3] He is fully aware of the impact those "double Ds" have on the male population and has made plenty of money by her refusal to cover them up. Ick.

In *The Body Project*, author Joan Jacobs Brumberg makes the thoughtful observation that "most Americans came to believe that a hallmark of Christian civilization was its ability to nurture and protect girlhood innocence: in effect, to guarantee a safe time between menarche and marriage, when girls would be sexually inactive. This principle influenced Victorian mothers in their dealings with developing daughters, and it animated countless community efforts to monitor and supervise young women in single-sex groups designed to promote innocence and purity."[4] Let's not forget that fifty years ago young women typically went through puberty later and married earlier. In addition there were stricter standards of dating and courtship during this time period, and it was common for parents to chaperone their children's coed activities.

Providing an Umbrella of Protection

In fact, I was recently reading an etiquette book that dates back to 1956, which I picked up in an antique store. In a chapter on manners, it addressed "conventions for the single woman living alone." Here is what it said: "There used to be only two conventionally acceptable ways for a marriageable young woman to live apart from her relatives: one was to live with a family who were friends of her parents, the other was to set up housekeeping in a respectable apartment house, complete with doorman, under the surveillance of an elderly servant chosen by her mother."[5] My, oh my, look at where we are some fifty years later! I share this not as a suggestion that we attempt to turn back the clocks of time but rather to illustrate the extent to which parents used to go to provide a safe umbrella of protection over their daughter until she had transitioned into marriage.

We are not excused today from providing our daughters with a new and updated "umbrella of protection" during the all too fleeting season of girlhood. As part of this effort, my husband and I have taken a few extra steps to provide additional protection for our daughter in her dating experiences. In addition to her dad having a talk with her first boyfriend, I also called and introduced myself to his mother. In the course of the conversation, I shared that one of the rules we feel strongly about is that Paige not spend time at this young man's house without a parent present (and our permission beforehand). We had the same rule for times when they were here in our home, and once we went upstairs to bed, he had to leave. In addition, we required that the young man come over to the house to pick Paige up even when they were planning to spend time at his house. At first she balked a bit at this requirement, but we explained that a little chivalry goes a long way. While we didn't expect him to break the bank taking her out on formal dates each time they got together, we did expect that he treat their informal get-togethers with the same level of respect. And finally, Paige and I have a long-standing date every couple of weeks where we go to dinner and talk about some of the more important matters, including her dating relationship. By keeping the lines of communication open, it sent the message that

> We are not excused today from providing our daughters with a new and updated "umbrella of protection" during the all too fleeting season of girlhood.

her father and I are engaged and will remain engaged in the process, as well we should be.

When I think about the call to provide an umbrella of protection over our daughters in regard to opposite sex relationships, I am reminded of Proverbs 4:23 which says, "Above all else, guard your heart, for it is the wellspring of life." Not only must we be diligent in setting up boundaries that aid in guarding our daughter's heart, but we must also be faithful in teaching our daughters to take the initiative to guard their own hearts. In the book *Raising Girls*, authors Melissa Trevathan and Sissy Goff address the balance of "gradually introducing your daughter into the world of boys" and yet also allowing her "enough freedom at home to be able to learn to make wise decisions regarding boys so that when she leaves home she can take that wisdom with her."[6] They note that "if a girl has no prior experience with boys, casual or otherwise, this danger can be compounded" when she leaves home. The authors also echo my belief that "it is helpful for her to have already had practice in this kind of decision making while she still lives under your roof," noting that "the best time for girls to make mistakes is while they are at home." They offer further wisdom in saying, "As she grows up, you can gradually widen the boundaries—giving her room to make her own decisions within the care of your watchful eye."[7] If we are having necessary conversations along the way with our daughters that outline a parent-approved model of dating, hopefully they will carry that same model and mind-set with them when they leave. Even for the girls who are not presented with an opportunity to date in the high school years, our words will not be wasted. We will have, at least, provided a framework for when the dating opportunity presents itself in God's timing.

Her first (and to date, only) dating experience has since ended, but overall it helped prepare her for other relationships that may come (and go) in the future.

College and Beyond: "Hanging Out" Versus "Going Out"

My husband and I have done our best to raise our boys to be well-mannered Southern gentlemen. You know, the ones who, much to the ire of feminists, race to open doors for women of all ages and allow them to pass through first, surrender their seats in waiting areas for women and children, keep an eye out for women and senior citizens who struggle to get their bags in the overhead bin when traveling (a particularly ouchy topic for me after logging so many travel hours and being this woman), and so on. I think you get the picture.

I share this background for the sake of revealing a downside to this hang-out-with-your-friends model that many Christian parents have endorsed in their homes (including me). As I was researching for this book, I began to see evidence of a trend where dating is all but extinct on college campuses, having been replaced by "hanging out" or "hooking up." I have written on this in the past in *Your Girl* and grieved that many of our daughters will fail to experience the excitement of an old-fashioned date. You know, the kind where the boy works up his nerve to call, drives over to pick up his date, takes his date out to dinner/movie and actually picks up the tab, and then politely drops his date off at her doorstep with no expectation of anything further. I can dream, right? As I was once again examining this trend, it dawned on me that I now have a college boy. And all of a sudden, I realized that I don't recall my son, Ryan (college boy) mentioning one single little date during his one and one-half years in college. So I picked up the phone and called college boy. Here, is a sampling of our conversation:

College boy: *(seeing my # on his phone)* Hey, Mom.

Me: Hey, son!

College boy: What's up?

Me: Oh, I was just writing about something in my book that I find disturbing, and I wanted to ask you something.

College boy: OK, shoot.

Me: So, is dating dead on college campuses?

College boy: Uh no, I don't think so.

Me: Really? Cuz I'm reading that most everyone just "hangs out" or "hooks up."

College boy: Yeah, people pretty much do that.

Me: OK, so let me ask you this: Have you been on any dates?

College boy: Uh, no, I guess not. *(hemming and hawing ensues)* I mean, the thing to do, ya know, is just hang out.

Me: Hmmm. So let me ask you this: Let's say you are hanging out with your group *(darling group, by the way, of Jesus-loving kids)*, and you meet a girl in the group and you think, *Wow, I might want to get to know her better.* So, what do you do?

College boy: Uh, well, I had that happen with one girl, so I just texted her later to see if she wanted to hang out and just come over and watch *The Office* or something.

Me: *(beginning to hyperventilate)* Wait a minute. Let me get this straight: You asked her to get in her car and drive over to your apartment to watch an episode of *The Office*? And then, at the end of the evening, she got into her car and drove her little self home *(insert sarcastic tone here)*?

College boy: Yeah, pretty much.

Me: *(praying out loud)* Lord Jesus, where did I go wrong? *(to son)* And at what point in the process do you ask her out on a real live date?

College boy: I don't know. Nobody really expects that.

Me: *(blood pressure rising)* What? Are you kidding me? *(Mom proceeds to launch into tirade where she grumbles about Christian girls letting Christian boys off the hook and male chivalry being near extinction. College boy responds by laughing.)*

And so how exactly did our conversation end? I can't even believe I'm about to confess this to you. I actually bribed my son and offered to foot the bill for a steak dinner for two if he would ask a girl out in the next two weeks. When I hung up, it hit me that his dad and I had, somehow, failed to address the topic of when it's appropriate to hang out and when it's appropriate to ask someone out. Sigh.

What really disturbs me is that when I talk to Christian girls about this, they say it's a huge catch-22. If they raise the bar higher and expect a boy to ask them out to get to know them, often the boy just moves on because there are plenty of girls who don't require such effort. Remember my own son's quote? "Nobody really expects that."

And the whole thing got me thinking. Have Christian parents gotten so carried away with this whole hang-out-in-groups model that we contribute to the problem when our kids carry it with them to their college years and beyond? Have we let our Christian boys off the hook by not expecting more of them? Do we go ahead and tell our daughters to raise the bar and wait for the rare boy whose mama raised him right (or bribed him with a steak dinner)? Now I will say in my son's defense that he later declined the steak-dinner-for-two bribery, arguing that he didn't want to lead someone on by asking her out unless he felt like there was a strong possibility that the date would lead to a relationship. And he refuses to enter a relationship unless he knows marriage is a good possibility down the road. I admired his explanation because, in today's world, that comes just about as close to courtship as you can get.

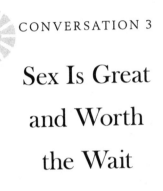

CONVERSATION 3

Sex Is Great
and Worth
the Wait

CHAPTER EIGHT

The Culture's Message:

Sex Is Great—Why Wait?

I was caught off guard one afternoon when my son (an eighth grader at the time) climbed into my car after school and began venting about a frustrating conversation he had during lunch that day. "Some of the girls in my grade are so messed up," he said with an air of disgust in his voice. He explained that he had been sitting with his friends at lunch, and two of the girls in the group broached the topic of sex. It's been awhile since I was in eighth grade, but I'm pretty certain sex was not on the list of acceptable lunch-table topics. It was understood that such topics as spin the bottle or rumors of so-and-so kissing so-and-so were saved for midnight ramblings at an all-girls' sleepover. Never would we imagine discussing such matters, especially sex, in the presence of boys.

My son explained that the conversation began when one "popular girl" posed the question, "What grade do you think you'll be in when you have sex in high school?" And thus the debate began as girls pondered whether they would lose their virginity in the ninth, tenth, or eleventh grade. Lovely, just lovely. Finally, my son said he could stand it no longer and piped up by suggesting the novel idea of waiting until marriage. And yes, you guessed it. He was laughed at, scorned, and shamed. "Hayden, no one waits until marriage! *Everyone* has sex in high school!" the girls responded. Hayden spoke up again and said, "Not my sister or brother. My brother's a freshman in college, and my sister's a junior in high school, and they're waiting until they get married." One girl chimed in, "Hayden, that's impossible. Trust me, they've had sex."

At this point, Hayden had reached his boiling point, and one of his friends, sensing his frustration, spoke up in his defense and said, "Hayden's sister is really good friends with my sister, and I'm pretty sure Hayden's right." At that point the girls speculated that perhaps his siblings were unattractive and, therefore, undesirable. The old "maybe something's wrong with them so no one wants them" explanation. What in the world could possibly explain two normal, run-of-the-mill teens running loose with their virginity still intact? Are they circus freaks, maybe?

And such is the world we live in. A world where Hollywood, hip-hop, and hibernating parents have left our kids thinking that sex is something you scratch off your to-do list by the tenth or eleventh grade with nothing more than a yawn or a shrug. I'm not sure what was more heartbreaking upon hearing my son's account of the lunchroom conversation that day: the warped attitudes among the eighth-grade girls at his lunch table or the fact that my son had been subjected to the warped attitudes among the eighth-grade girls at his lunch table. In the end I concluded that at the very least it helped him find his voice and stand up for his beliefs. He has since entered high school and I can only pray that he will remain strong in his convictions even when his hormones are raging out of control and casting a vote to "go for it." Clearly, some of the girls have marked their calendars.

C'mon, Everyone's Doing It!

If I had to sum up the culture's message regarding sex, it would match a customer review on Amazon for one of my books to teen girls. Apparently my suggestion that God created sex for the confines of marriage didn't sit well with one reader who gave my book a one star review and offered the following comments: "90 percent of world's population will have sex before they are married. . . . People will always want to have sex; it's human nature!"

Unfortunately, she failed to include the Scripture verse where she gleaned that wisdom—oh but wait, there's *not* one. While I would agree with her that it is human nature to want to have sex, I'm not sure I follow her logic when she assumes that because 90 percent of the world's population will have sex before they are married, it must therefore be OK. The majority of Americans are also in debt and overweight, so I guess that's OK too? And I wonder if 90 percent of the population jumped off a bridge if the reader above would join them?

Perhaps God created us with a "human nature" to want to have sex in order that it might be enjoyed in marriage and serve as a means to procreate the world. And perhaps 90 percent of the population has failed to follow His game plan for sex, opting instead to write their own rules for the game. When it comes to sex, the rules of the world's game are simple: Sex is OK as long as it's mutual and protected. Go for it! Just *be safe*. Your daughter will hear that message over and over again, compliments of the sexual revolution spawned by the original women's libber "girl power" movement of the 1960s and 1970s.

Feminists were outraged that women were so sexually repressed (translation: sex was only accepted in marriage) and began to rally for the same perks typically enjoyed by men: sex on demand with no strings attached. And here we are today, some forty to fifty years later, and they have their wish. The men, of course, were more than happy along the way to oblige the women in their quest for sexual liberation, and today we are experiencing the fruits of girl power. The only problem is, the fruit is rotten, but in spite of this obvious evidence, the free sex message continues to thrive. In fact, it only gets worse.

> **W**hen it comes to sex, the rules of the world's game are simple: Sex is OK as long as it's mutual and protected. Go for it! Just *be safe.*

Sex Sells

It's nearly impossible to watch a half hour of TV without being force-fed the "sex sells" message, whether it's an ad for a bag of Doritos or Axe Deodorant (the latter, interestingly, owned by Unilever, which is the same company behind Dove's Campaign for Real Beauty ads). I dare you to surf through your one hundred plus cable or satellite stations and count the number of times women are being objectified or sold the hook-up lie.

During the course of writing this chapter, I happened to tune into a *Sex in the City* rerun out of pure curiosity. Within five minutes, I had a lump in my throat and felt sick to my stomach. The focus of the show was, of course, the rampant hook-up sex the main characters experience. One of the main characters, Miranda, discovers she has chlamydia and is forced to tally up all the men she has slept with in order to notify them that they may be carriers. As she's scribbling down name after name on a piece of paper, she expresses amazement that she somehow managed to get through law school, graduate with honors, and become a successful attorney in spite of the frequency of her little sex-tracurricular activity. Later, in a scene where she is in bed with her boyfriend, she refers to herself as a "dirty, diseased whore" and expresses concern that the list she made of her past sexual partners wasn't a short one. He questions her about the number, and with some prodding she admits that she has slept with forty-two different men. He follows by admitting to sleeping with more than sixty women.

Meanwhile, another character, Carrie Bradshaw, played by Sarah Jessica Parker, is confused as to why her new love interest of just ten days has not accepted her invitation to spend the night (translation: have sex). After she confronts him and boldly asks for a reason, he explains that it's just been ten days and after sleeping casually with so many different women, he is trying to move in the direction of saving sex for someone he truly cares for. As her date kisses her at the door and walks away, she ponders this unpredicted shift from *sex* to *romance* (which caught her off guard) and didn't even enter her mind as a possibility in a relationship. She concludes her thoughts with the classic statement, "Are we simply romantically challenged, or are we sluts?" Am I allowed to answer that?

Typically the shows that are popular among teen girls and young women are shows that peddle hookups and brazen sexuality as the norm. If you are a virgin, you are a freak. Many girls will buy into this lie and seek to emulate what they see played out on the screen for fear that the alternative is dreadfully old-fashioned. Casual hookups and FWBs (friends with benefits) are so common that most every teen girl knows someone who has hooked up just for the fun of it. Girl power at its finest. And why wouldn't they want to hook up? They see it on just about every show they watch, and it's portrayed as chic and empowering. No strings attached. No phone call the next morning. No relationship drama. And best of all, you are in control—all pleasure and no obligations. But are you really in control? Seems to me that you lose much of your bargaining power when you give the guys something for nothing. Dawn Eden, author of *The Thrill of the Chaste: Finding Fulfillment While Keeping Your Clothes On*, says, "In this bizarre alternate universe—which, sadly, has become reality for many of today's youth—good and evil themselves are redefined. No longer is it bad to allow oneself to use and be used sexually. The only sin is failing to 'protect' yourself by using a condom or other form of contraception."[1]

> Hookups (friends with benefits) are so common that almost every teen girl knows someone who has hooked up just for the fun of it.

Oh, but wait, I'm so confused. Did that come in the liberation bundle pack? I've already ranted about the degrading song lyrics that are all too common in hip-hop/rock music in chapter 3. It used to be that the only girls flashing their breasts and privates were Playboy models or strip club dancers. Today girls flash their privates for free whether it's pantieless pop stars like Britney, who has upped the ante on what constitutes shock value, or college girls lifting their shirts on the beach for a *Girls Gone Wild* video. And who needs the videos when the average girl next door is willing to expose herself on a whim (and usually under the influence) for a friend's digital camera? They hardly flinch when the picture is posted to one of their friends' MySpace or Facebook pages. Sadly, it's just par for the course nowadays.

Try as we may, it is nearly impossible to protect our daughter from the media onslaught that will vie for her attention when it comes to sexual promiscuity. And some parents, I dare say, are not even trying. Would you believe that a survey in 2005 found that

Desperate Housewives ranked as the most popular network television show among kids ages nine to twelve? No wonder sex outside of marriage doesn't even make the radar on the list of immoral deeds among the youth of today.[2] We live in a culture where girls hardly raise an eyebrow when a friend admits to hooking up the night before. College girls have taken to signing up for pole-dancing classes, and teen girls shop at Victoria's Secret for lacy lingerie that was once reserved for the wedding night. Our hyper-sexualized culture has had an impact on our girls, and to remain silent and wish it away will do even more harm.

Ignorance Is Not Bliss

What I'm about to say will discourage some of you and make others of you angry, but I'm going to say it anyway. I am not saying this for shock value but rather to serve as a wake-up call and move us past the ignorance that says, "Not my precious angel—she has virgin written all over her." Given the current statistics regarding the percentage of girls having sex outside of marriage, the majority of our daughters will not make it to their wedding night with their purity intact. Whew, I said it. How do I know this? Take a look at the statistics:

Number of females reporting they've had vaginal intercourse:

26 percent of fifteen-year-olds

40 percent of sixteen-year-olds

49 percent of seventeen-year-olds

70 percent of eighteen-year-olds

77 percent of nineteen-year-olds

92 percent of twenty-two- to twenty-four-year-olds[3]

I should note that the statistics above also include married females who fall into the age ranges, so it would include some females who may have remained chaste until marriage. Another study found that 80 percent of college students (18 to 24 years of age) have engaged in sexual intercourse.[4] Further, a survey in 2002 of about 12,500 men and women found that 97 percent of those they surveyed who were "no longer virgins at age 44 had sexual intercourse for the first time before they married."[5]

But wait, it gets worse. Another study found that the average number of sex partners for men is twenty and the average number for women is six.[6] And before we jump to conclusions about the purity of past generations, here is an interesting finding: Among women born between 1939 and 1948, 48 percent reported having had premarital intercourse by age twenty. That number increased to 65 percent for women born between 1949 and 1958 (representing the teens of the free-love movement originating in the 1960s. Among the women born between 1959 and 1968, those reporting premarital sex by age twenty was 72 percent, and for those born between 1969 and 1978, the figure was 76 percent.[7]

Is the virgin bride a thing of the past, so rare that girls are unable even to recount one girlfriend who defied the odds, themselves included? It certainly brings new meaning to Proverbs 31:10 which says, "Who can find a virtuous woman? for her worth is far above rubies" (KJV). Most of us (myself included) would like to believe our precious girls will be among the virtuous and virgin elite, but the truth is, many will cave into the pressure. When you mix the culture's message, that sex is natural, with the hormone factor, there is little to hold them back.

> Is the virgin bride a thing of the past, so rare that girls are unable even to recount one girlfriend who defied the odds, themselves included?

Nowadays a girl is considered fairly exceptional if she can make it to her wedding day with less than three sexual partners or commit herself to secondary virginity at some point. I've even heard of a trend among couples to abstain from sex for a brief time before the wedding in an attempt to make it more special. Is this as good as it gets?

While I was not a virgin bride on my wedding day, my husband and I waited to have sex until we were married. My husband was a virgin, and I was a fairly new believer and had committed myself to secondary virginity. We just celebrated another anniversary, and I can still remember to this day how exciting it was to wait until we were married. We still laugh about how I would stare at him while he was sleeping. I could hardly believe that each and every morning I would get to wake up next to this wonderful man. As I replay that feeling of excitement over the novelty of becoming one after we were married rather than before, it's hard for me to understand what the thrill is for the couple who has already shared a bed before saying "I do." Surely it must be a letdown, especially for the couples who have lived together for quite some time.

God knew what He was doing when He created sex for the confines of marriage. It's up to us to educate our daughters to the why behind His rules. No doubt we have our work cut out for us. I didn't write this chapter to depress you, but rather to implore you to address the two-ton elephant that's sitting in the middle of the room. We must have some candid and blunt conversations with our daughters to arm them in the battle they face. It can't be ignored any longer. The culture is screaming for your daughter's attention. Is she listening?

"He feeds on ashes, a deluded heart misleads him; he cannot save himself, or say, 'Is not this thing in my right hand a lie?'" (Isa. 44:20)

CHAPTER NINE

What the Culture Is NOT Telling Your Daughter about Sex

Your daughter is bombarded with messages regarding sex on a daily basis. The general message is that sex is a sign of girl power, signifying strength and independence. Unfortunately, our girls are not being told the whole story. When was the last time you saw a scene on TV or in a movie that, after highlighting sex outside of marriage, showed one of the characters dealing with depression over a tattered reputation due to promiscuity? Or how about dealing with an unwanted pregnancy? Or what about the aftermath of abortion where depression and regret are commonly experienced? What if the media reflected the reality that one-fourth of all teen girls has an STD and allowed one-fourth of their female characters to contract an STD? What if the media portrayed the fallout from contracting an STD—like working up your nerve to tell your partner or, for that matter, your future partners?

Of course, our girls won't see reality because it doesn't line up with the girl power message the culture is preaching. So the lie continues to be peddled day in and day out, leaving our girls with the impression that sex is nothing more than a recreational hobby. No consequences, no strings attached. But there *are* consequences, and there *are* strings attached, but no one has the guts to say it. The real paradox is that, in the end, sexual freedom and this girl-power-run-amok movement have left our girls powerless and reduced them to nothing more than objects for the male viewing pleasure. Some freedom.

The Good News First: The Rewards of Waiting

In addition to ignoring the fallout from having sex outside of marriage, the media also fails to address the benefits of saving sex for marriage. Think about it. When was the last time you heard a media report announcing that those who abstain from sex outside of marriage have the best sex once they are married? The Family Research Council surveyed eleven hundred people about their sexual satisfaction and found that 72 percent of all married "traditionalists" (those who "strongly believe out of wedlock sex is wrong") reported a higher sexual satisfaction. "Traditionalists" scored roughly thirty-one percentage points higher than the level registered by unmarried "nontraditionalists" (those who have no or only some objection to sex outside of marriage) and thirteen percentage points higher than married nontraditionalists.[1]

It gets better. Another study by the National Institute for Healthcare Research found that "strictly monogamous women experienced orgasm during sex more than twice as often as promiscuous women."[2] Researcher David Larson said that couples who don't sleep together before marriage and who are faithful during marriage are more satisfied with their current sex life and also with their marriages compared to those who were involved sexually before marriage.[3]

And the perks don't stop there. Several researchers with the Heritage Foundation analyzed data from the 1995 National Survey of Family Growth and found that for women thirty or older, those who were monogamous (only one sexual partner in a lifetime) were by far most likely to be still in a stable relationship (80 percent). Sleeping with just one extra partner dropped that probability to 54 percent. Two extra partners brought it down to 44 percent.[4] Clearly, there is a link between self-restraint practiced before marriage and a lasting and fruitful marriage. Most of our girls would admit to wanting a healthy and happy marriage as a long-term goal. I wonder how many might alter their behavior and choose to abstain if they knew that, in doing so, they would greatly increase their likelihood of remaining in a lasting, monogamous marriage.

Let me put this into perspective. Here is the exact conversation I had with my own daughter to illustrate this powerful finding. "Paige, if you line up ten of your friends who have already had two or more sexual partners, approximately six will be divorced by their twentieth high school reunion. However, if you line up ten girls who successfully abstain from sex prior to marriage (of which I hope you will be one), only two will be divorced by their twentieth high school reunion. In other words, if you sleep with just two guys prior to marriage, you will be three times more likely to divorce than if you abstain."[5] In addition, I pointed out to my daughter that those who remain married will make better parents and have a higher likelihood of raising happy children. The decision to have sex outside of marriage can literally be a predictor of future fallout in a young woman's life. Is the momentary pleasure gained from sex outside of marriage really worth risking future happiness? Ironically the media will highlight the importance of family but continue to ignore the above-mentioned findings that, if practiced, increase the likelihood of having a happy and healthy family.

Of course, you don't hear the media highlighting any of the above data. The culture will continue to tell our daughters that sex is a natural, normal part of life. They will scream and fight to abolish abstinence-based sex education and continue to peddle the "safe sex" message ad nauseam. It is imperative that we as mothers pick up the slack and share with our daughters the details that the culture refuses to address. I honestly cannot imagine that most girls, including those with no religious foundation or affiliation, wouldn't appreciate being fully informed before making such a life-altering decision.

Now, the Bad News: The Fallout from Not Waiting

Unless we expose the faulty thinking behind the culture's free-sex message and the fallout that has resulted from believing it, it will be impossible to adequately address the issue of sex outside of marriage with our daughters. It's not enough to tell our daughters to "wait because God says so." They deserve to know all the facts before making a decision to have sex outside of marriage. By the time you finish this chapter, I imagine that like me, you will be shrugging your shoulders in disbelief over how this lie can continue when the fallout from having sex outside of marriage is so evident. Granted, I realize that our daughters are hardly being

> It's not enough to tell our daughters to "wait because God says so."

told the truth about the fallout; therefore it's up to us to inform them.

Perhaps one of the most ironic factors regarding the culture's message that girls should pursue sexual freedom is that almost half (41 percent) of girls ages fourteen to seventeen reported having "unwanted sex" because they feared their partner would get angry if denied sex.[6] Another study found that even when the sex is wanted, it is often soon regretted. In fact, the National Campaign to Prevent Teen Pregnancy in 2004 found that two-thirds of all sexually experienced teens said that they wished they had waited longer before having sex.[7]

Dawn Eden, author of the book *The Thrill of the Chaste: Finding Fulfillment While Keeping Your Clothes On*, admits that her pursuit of sexual freedom left her feeling anything but free. She confessed, "When I sought sexual experiences with men, it was as a distraction from the emptiness I felt inside."[8] The more I examine the mounting evidence that sex outside of marriage has a negative impact on the physical, emotional, and spiritual development of young women, the more I understand God's wisdom in 1 Corinthians 6:13: "The body is not meant for sexual immorality, but for the Lord, and the Lord for the body." After reading the evidence below, I'm sure you'll agree that abstaining until marriage simply makes logical sense. Get your highlighters out and let's examine the facts.

After the Hookup

While I was writing this chapter, FoxNews.com ran the following article: "Friends with Benefits a Bum Deal?" I'm sure you'll find this as no surprise, but apparently girls have a hard time emotionally detaching themselves in a friends with benefits relationship. The article states, "Contrary to popular belief, having a friend with benefits may not be all it's cracked up to be."[9] Really?

A Michigan study found "that friends with benefits relationships often reach the point where one friend starts to develop feelings for the other, but only one-tenth of these arrangements actually end in a full-scale romance and unreciprocated feelings can lead to the demise of the friendship."[10] Well, no duh. So much for the touted "no strings attached" perk that the culture promises in the hook-up package. Could it be that we are wired in such a way that sex connects us on a deeper level in spite of any desire we may have on our part to pursue it for physical pleasure alone? The article concludes, "Turns out that, despite the conveniences of FWBs, temporary sexual gratification comes at a price—the chance at real romance."[11]

A separate study sponsored by the Independent Women's Forum called "Hooking Up, Hanging Out, and Hoping for Mr. Right" further proved that our free sex culture is not without heavy emotional consequences. The study found an alarming trend of young people hooking up for casual sex without any promise of commitment or long-term relationships. The report was based on surveys of college women who all but confirmed that traditional dating is a thing of the past. The independence and empowerment promised to women by the sexual revolution as a result of no-commitment hookups has left young women feeling anything but empowered. In fact, 61 percent of survey respondents said that a hookup makes them feel "desirable" but also "awkward."[12] Here is further proof that it is nearly impossible to detach yourself emotionally from the physical act of sex. One Princeton grad summed it up this way: "The whole thing is a very male-dominated scene. Hooking up lets men get physical pleasure without any emotional connection, but for the women it's hard to separate the physical from the emotional. Women want the call the next day."[13]

Double Standard: Guys Are Studs, Girls Are Skanks . . . Some Things Never Change

Someone recently sent me a link to a Facebook group a guy had set up called, "Krisha is a slut." For those not familiar with Facebook, it is a social networking site that is popular among teens. In addition to setting up a personal profile page, it offers teens the ability to create groups and invite their friends to join their group. The average friend list numbers in the hundreds so you can imagine the viral impact of this upgraded version of the gossip game. Here is a description of the "Krisha is a slut" group:

> So, it's realllllly aparrent, and rather blatantly obvious that Krisha is a huge slut and this is just a group to show that Krisha is the biggest slut, whore, ho, trick, tramp, broad, prostitute, hooker, skank, floozy, hussy, nymphomaniac, sperm-loving, sex-having, "person" that we know.

In the comments feature, many guys had posted comments pertaining to their own hook-up experience with Krisha. Shocked? Don't be. This is an everyday occurrence on the social networking sites. Locker room talk has now expanded to the World Wide Web. In *Teenage Girls: Exploring Issues Adolescent Girls Face and Strategies to Help Them*, author Ginny Olson noted, "Girls are well aware that there's a fine line between having 'status sex' (the kind that raises their social capital) and 'slut sex' (i.e., having too much sex with too many partners and ultimately lowering their social capital). When the latter hap-

Locker room talk has now expanded to the World Wide Web.

pens, they may be branded 'slut,' 'skank,' 'bitch,' or 'hoe,' which is in marked contrast to a guy who exhibits the same behavior and gets endowed with the title 'player.'"[14]

One teen boy confirms the above:

> Dear Abby: I'm a guy, 18, and I have something to say to girls who sleep around. They may think they are "hot stuff," but they should hear what is said about them in the locker room. These poor girls think it is flattering to be sought out—that it is a compliment to have sex. Not so! It is cheap and degrading to be used.[15]

In a survey by *Seventeen* magazine, 91 percent of teens agreed with this statement: "A girl can get a bad reputation if she has sex." In the same survey, 92 percent of teens agreed with the statement: "It is generally considered a good thing for a girl to be a virgin."[16] Girls may think that the boys will like them more if they have sex, but in reality boys respect the girls who choose to save sex for marriage. Some things never change.

Oxytocin: the Bonding Effect

Did you know that neuroscientists have discovered a chemical that is involved in the bonding process? The chemical is called oxytocin and it's a hormone that acts as a messenger from one organ to another. It has been linked as the hormone that is sent from the brain to the uterus and breasts to induce labor, as well as to let down milk after the baby is born. But here's where it gets interesting. It has been discovered that oxytocin is also released during sexual activity.[17] Author of *Unprotected: A Campus Psychiatrist Reveals How Political Correctness in Her Profession Endangers Every Student*, Anonymous, M.D, asks, "Could it be that the same chemical that flows through a woman's veins as she nurses her infant, promoting a powerful and selfless devotion is found in college women 'hooking up' with men whose last intention is to bond?"[18] Interestingly, it has also been discovered that in addition to bonding, oxytocin increases trust.[19] Trust, no doubt, intended between a newborn and a mother or a husband and wife.

Psychologist Jess Lair, of Montana State University, describes the bonding process that takes place during sexual intercourse in this way: "Sexual bonding includes powerful emotional, psychological, physical, and spiritual links that are so strong that the two people become one, at least for a moment. Sexual intercourse is an intense, though brief physical bonding that leaves indelible marks on the participants. . . . To believe one can walk away from a sexual experience untouched is dangerously naïve."[20]

> To believe one can walk away from a sexual experience untouched is dangerously naïve.

Dawn Eden in *The Thrill of the Chaste* describes the conflict of emotions that occurs after hooking up that lends support to the oxytocin research. She says:

When I was having casual sex, there was one moment I dreaded more than any other. I dreaded it not out of fear that the sex would be bad, but out of fear that it would be good. If the sex was good, then, even if I knew in my heart that the relationship wouldn't work, I would still feel as though the act had bonded me with my sex partner in a deeper way than we had been bonded before. It's in the nature of sex to awaken deep emotions within us— emotions that are distinctly unwelcome when one is trying to keep it light. At such times, the worst moment was when it was all over. Suddenly, I was jarred back to earth.

Then I'd lie back and feel . . . bereft. My partner was still there, and if I was really lucky, he'd lie down next to me. Yet, I couldn't help feeling like the spell had been broken. We could nuzzle or giggle, or we could fall asleep in each other's arms, but I knew I was playacting—and so did my partner. We weren't really intimate—it had just been a game. The circus had left town.[21]

It's hard for me to imagine how any girl or young woman would not think twice about having sex outside of marriage once they are informed of the bonding aspect that has been proven with oxytocin. I can't help but wonder if perhaps it would have impacted my decision as a teen girl. Of course, for a girl who thinks she is in love, "bonding" sounds like a positive rather than a negative. For me personally, it explains so much of my attachment to my high school boyfriend after we became sexually active. Jealousy, insecurity, and an overall possessiveness entered our relationship. Once physical intimacies have been exchanged, pulling back from the relationship is difficult and recovering when a breakup occurs is even more difficult than for those who did not swap physical intimacies.

Increased Risk for Depression and Suicide

Numerous studies have noted an increase in depression among sexually active girls. The National Longitudinal Survey of Adolescent Health found that 25.3 percent of sexually active girls ages fourteen to seventeen reported that they felt depressed "a lot of the time" or "most all of the time," as compared with 7.7 percent who were not sexually active.[22] Another study of sixty-five hundred adolescents found that sexually active teenage girls were more than three times as likely to be depressed and nearly three times as likely to have had a suicide attempt than girls who were not sexually active.[23]

If you ever doubted that girls have a harder time separating their emotions from the physical act of sex, another study published in the *Journal of Health and Social Behavior* analyzed the data on eight thousand teens and found that "females experience a larger increase in depression than males in response to romantic involvement," and that "females' greater vulnerability to romantic involvement may explain the higher rates of depression in female teens."[24]

Obviously the evidence continues to mount, yet stop and think about it. How often do you recall the media exposing the results of these reputable studies? It amazes me that you can find warning labels on just about everything imaginable, yet when it comes to warning our young women about side effects linked to out of wedlock sex, such as depression (among many others), mum's the word. Even the medical community is encouraged to remain silent lest they infringe upon a young woman's personal choice. No doubt they would speak up should a young patient admit to smoking. They would likely launch into a lecture regarding the dangers associated with smoking and the increased risk for lung cancer and emphysema. Yet culture's only concern seems to be with protection from STDs and unplanned pregnancies. Unfortunately, condoms and birth control pills can't protect the psyche.

STDs and Infertility

Perhaps you remember the rumblings in the news regarding a study from the Centers for Disease Control that found at least one in four teenage girls nationwide has a sexually transmitted disease (STD). The study found that nearly half the girls in their sample were sexually active and among those, 40 percent tested positive for an STD.[25] Sigh. No, make that a heavy sign.

Some STDs are incurable, and others can hinder or even prevent young women from someday bearing children. Worse yet, consider the human papillomavirus or HPV, which can lead to cervical cancer. According to the Centers for Disease Control, approximately twenty million people are currently infected with HPV. At least 50 percent of sexually active men and women acquire genital HPV infection at some point in their lives. By age fifty, at least 80 percent of women will have acquired genital HPV infection. About 6.2 million Americans get a new genital HPV infection each year. Most HPV infections have no signs or symptoms; therefore, most infected persons are unaware they are infected, yet they can transmit the virus to a sex partner.[26]

And then there's chlamydia. According to the Centers for Disease Control, chlamydia remains the most commonly reported infectious disease in the United States. In 2003, 877,478 chlamydial infections were reported to CDC, up from 834,555 cases reported in 2002. Because many cases are not reported or even diagnosed, it is estimated that there are actually 2.8 million new cases of chlamydia each year.[27] Additionally, a report from 2005 found that nearly one in twenty women between the ages of fourteen and nineteen (4.6 percent) were infected, the highest proportion of any age group.[28]

An anonymous physician at a large university health center, penned the book *Unprotected: A Campus Psychiatrist Reveals How Political Correctness in Her Profession Endangers Every Student*, has been sounding the alarm for some time about chlamydia:

> We do know that most women who have been infected discover it in a startling way—when they can't conceive. Since in up to 80 percent of infected women, Chlamydia produces no pain, fever, or discharge, a woman thinks she's fine. Like her infected cells, she's an unsuspecting hostess to a dangerous guest. Years later, when she's settled down, married, and put the partying and hookups

behind her; she's told that her blood has antichlamydial antibodies—evidence of an old infection. The doctor puts a scope through her navel to look at her fallopian tubes, and discovers they are enlarged and scarred by adhesions. And this is the reason she cannot have a baby.[29]

She further notes that risk factors that lead to chlamydia are intercourse at an early age, many partners, and possibly even the use of oral contraceptives.[30]

In addition, the author makes the following observation that should serve as a wake-up call to every mother reading this that we are on our own when it comes to informing our daughters of the dangers that can come from STDs. She brilliantly compares how the *Journal of American College Health* sees the issue of osteoporosis prevention to that of infertility that can result from STDs. Here is what the journal says in regard to osteoporosis:

> College students of all ages deserve to be educated about the risk factors that lead to osteoporosis. Young women, in particular, need to be informed about how proper nutrition and regular exercise can help them achieve optimal peak bone mass. They need to be aware that a diet low in calcium and vitamin D as well as smoking, alcohol abuse, steroid use, high-protein diets, and both physical inactivity and excessive exercise may have a negative impact on the lifetime health of their bone structure and may predispose them to a higher risk of osteoporosis in later years.[31]

What does this same journal have to say about infertility that can result from STDs? Nothing. Nada. Not even a peep. Our anonymous campus physician asks this question: "If there is a need to educate a twenty-something-year-old woman about the prevention of a postmenopausal condition, is there not an equal or greater need to make sure she's well-informed about fertility? Given that many college women postpone childbearing longer than ever, and others expose themselves to genital bacteria and viruses, one might wonder why we don't find a warning of this sort in the campus health literature."[32] This sort of political correctness run amok is enough to make your blood boil. This brave M.D. confessed to writing this book after being hushed time and time again in attempts to share the risks associated with sex with the students visiting her clinic. Mothers, clearly the burden is on us to pass along this vital information to our daughters so they can make a truly informed decision.

CHAPTER TEN

Teen Pregnancy: Being Honest about the Options

Believe it or not, more than 40 percent of young women in the United States become pregnant one or more times before they reach twenty years of age.[1] Of those pregnancies, about four-fifths are unintended. Approximately 15 percent of all teen pregnancies end in miscarriages, 29 percent end in legal abortions, and 55 percent end in births.[2] Given that nearly one in two girls will find themselves pregnant in

> More than 40 percent of young women in the United States become pregnant one or more times before they reach twenty years of age.

their teen years, I feel it's necessary for mothers to engage their daughters in honest and candid conversations regarding the options available.

While we hope that our daughters will not have to experience the consequences arising from an unexpected teen pregnancy, it would be naïve to believe they are exempt. Even if they make wise choices, chances are they will know someone who is represented in the nearly 40 percent of teen girls who become pregnant. The purpose in presenting the information below is twofold: first, to equip your daughter with biblical truth regarding the options touted by culture and second, to equip your daughter with biblical truth that she can, in turn, pass along to a friend in need.

Abortion

She was barely seventeen when she went in for her "procedure." No one knew she was pregnant except her boyfriend and a coworker who had recommended the clinic. She was pro-choice, so it was a no-brainer of a decision. She was a junior and on the varsity cheerleading squad with plans to attend college after graduation. Her boyfriend seemed to struggle more with the decision, as it was hard to reconcile with his Catholic upbringing. However, he agreed that there was no other viable alternative. He was a graduating senior and had been awarded a soccer scholarship at a prestigious university. They called the clinic and felt relieved when a date was on the calendar.

On the morning of the appointment, her coworker called the high school and pretended to be her mother and informed them that she was ill and would not be in school that day. Her boyfriend normally drove her to school in the mornings, so parents didn't suspect a thing when he pulled into the driveway on that morning in November. Little was said during the twenty-mile drive to the clinic on the outskirts of town. He seemed to be focused on the directions to ensure that they didn't get lost. She fumbled with the radio, looking for anything to distract her from thinking about the *procedure*. She couldn't even bring herself to say the word in her mind.

Finally they arrived. As they entered the waiting room, she noticed several other girls that appeared to be close to her age, some alone and a few with their boyfriends. Another girl, who was clearly much younger, sat stoically next to her mother. She wondered for a moment about their stories. She checked in at the window and was immediately handed a mound of paperwork. Her boyfriend settled the bill, paying $250 in cash. After filling out the paperwork, she and her boyfriend passed the time by playing hangman and tic-tac-toe on a scratch sheet of paper. The wait in the waiting room seemed like forever when in actuality it was less than a half hour.

Finally, she was startled when she heard her name called by a nurse standing in the doorway of the waiting room. She stood and briefly looked back at her boyfriend. He gave her a gentle nod of reassurance as she walked toward the nurse. She didn't look back again as she walked through the doorway and was ushered down a narrow corridor. After a blood test and a brief meeting with a nurse to confirm her decision to move forward with the *procedure*, she was led into a cold and sterile room.

The details after that were a blur, gray and devoid of detail. A brief introduction by a doctor in a white lab coat. A friendly nurse who held her hand as the anesthesia was administered. Then nothing. Her next memory is waking up in a larger room with many beds, each closed off by curtains. She was alone for a few minutes until a nurse came to her side and informed her that she was in recovery.

The nurse asked her if she had brought anyone with her and if so, would she like for her friend to join her in the recovery room? She nodded her head and softly gave her boyfriend's name. She was not in any pain, but her mind was racing. She began to cry softly. She didn't want to call attention to herself, so she tried to muffle her sobs by turning her head into her pillow. She had thought she would have felt nothing but sheer relief, so the tears caught her off guard. When she looked up, her boyfriend was at her side. He seemed uncertain as to how to respond to her sadness. He fidgeted nervously and leaned down and whispered, "We'll be out of here soon." His words brought little comfort, and she remembers just *wanting her mother.* She was seventeen years old, and she needed her mother. But her mother didn't know. They had agreed not to tell anyone. In fact, they agreed to never acknowledge that it happened. It was time to move on.

By the end of the week, she was cheering at the football game and back into her normal routine. She and her boyfriend would continue to date for another couple of years. She never doubted her decision to have the *procedure*, but from time to time, she would be caught off guard by a sudden remembrance. There was the time when she was a sophomore in college and had gone to her younger cousin's soccer game. She was sitting in the bleachers watching a group of five-year-old boys as they ran down the field in pursuit of the ball. Suddenly, she was overcome by an overwhelming sense of sadness. She had always thought that the baby had been a boy and somehow seeing these young boys made her wonder about her baby and what might have been.

She was staunchly pro-choice and had become more so in the years that had followed her abortion. It had brought her comfort to know that it was nothing more than a blob of tissue, but on this particular day, as she watched the boys running up and down the field, she had to wonder. *Would her boy be about the same age as these boys? Would he have played soccer?* Where did that come from? She felt warm pools of tears forming in her eyes as she fought back the unwelcome thoughts. She quickly got up and made a getaway to her car before her tears were noticed. As she sat in her car and watched the boys play from afar, she wept aloud and wondered if perhaps what she had done was *wrong*. Even she was shocked by what came out of her mouth next. "Oh my God. What have I done?"

I am all too familiar with the pain that can surface unexpectedly, years after an abortion. The story above is *my story*. The guilt and shame continued to plague me that following year. It was as if a button had been pushed, and suddenly a floodgate of pent-up emotions had come to the surface. In the summer after my junior year of college, a friend would invite me to a Christian retreat for college students being held over the Labor Day weekend. I responded to the gospel of Jesus Christ after hearing about the offer of God's forgiveness. The abortion was forefront in my mind that evening when I bowed my head and prayed. I welcomed this forgiveness and a new life that was being offered.

It would take another decade (and a bit of counseling) for me finally to accept that God had forgiven me for the abortion. By that time I had married and had three children. Each pregnancy and birth experience served as further confirmation that abortion is anything but a quick fix and every child is, in fact, a gift from God. Today God has done a mighty work in my life, and I am no longer in bondage to the shame. I have shared the testimony of my past abortion on occasion in speaking engagements but never in detail as I have done above. My children know about the abortion, and I plan to allow them to read the detailed account. I realize that more than one in three women reading this right now has also experienced an abortion. The Alan Guttmacher Institute has determined that by age

> The Alan Guttmacher Institute has determined that by age forty-five, one out of every 2.5 women in the U.S. has had at least one abortion.

forty-five, one out of every 2.5 women in the U.S. has had at least one abortion.[3]

Anything but a Quick Fix

I am discouraged that over two decades have passed since my abortion and women today are still not being told the whole truth when it comes to abortion. It continues to be peddled as a "quick fix" solution to enable a woman to move on with her life. Yet the truth is, most women are unable to have the procedure and put it out of their minds from that point forward. In fact, the Guttmacher study above found that with the passing of time, negative emotions like sadness and regret increased, and decision satisfaction decreased. That is, more women reported sadness and regret two years following an abortion than one month after the event.[4]

One look at the bulletin boards on a popular site for women who have experienced abortion (www.afterabortion.com) will confirm that the above is true. Mind you, this is not a religiously affiliated site, and thus it attracts women of all ages, stages, and beliefs to share their stories or seek advice. Examples of the subject line in just a week's worth of threads include words or phrases such as: *"guilt; regret; will I always feel this way?; what bothers me the most; I feel lost and I hurt so bad; tired of faking it; does it ever get better?; my sister is pregnant and it makes me feel sad; I just want it to stop so I can move on; I'm 16 and I'm sad; tell me how to forget; sad today; so alone; I'm crashing; I feel like I'm dying; getting worse; help; I want to be with my baby; this would have been my baby's first Christmas."*

When I clicked through on some of the threads, I found heart-wrenching grief expressed by women of all ages. Here are some examples:

I know that this is ultimately for the best but I miss the

baby inside of me. I feel horrible and cry all the time. I blame myself for everything. I wish I could take back what I did, but I can't.

I had one more chance to see my baby on the screen and I couldn't look. I let her down by not looking at her. I can't believe I don't have her anymore. How could I do that to her?

I just can't ever live the same way again. Nothing will ever feel normal again.

After I woke up from my abortion, I cried and begged the nurse to give me my baby back.[5]

Over and over again, women speak of triggering experiences or events that bring their loss to the surface. My cousin's soccer game had been a triggering event for me. Interestingly, I could not find one woman on the boards who referred to a "mass of tissue" or a "fetus." They each spoke of a "baby," and because of the advancement of technology, some knew the sex of their child from the ultrasound performed prior to the procedure to confirm the stage of fetal development. Some women regretted looking at the image while others were pondering getting the medical records so they could see their baby one more time. I wept as I read the accounts and the desperate cries for help. Many expressed shock and even surprise over the emotional pain they were experiencing. They had expected to feel an immediate relief after the abortion, yet relief was nowhere in sight—only sadness and despair.

In addition to feeling sadness when reading the women's comments, I also felt intense anger. Anger over the fact that so many women have been duped and lied to over the years, led to believe it would "fix" the problem. Essentially, all they did was trade one perceived "problem" for an even bigger one. Mind you, many of these women posting on the boards call themselves "pro-choice" and, in their honesty, wrestle with believing they did the right thing while at the same time feeling a tremendous loss. I couldn't help but wonder if the best way to cut down on abortions would be to route women who are considering having one to visit www.afterabortion. com before they decide in order to hear firsthand accounts from women who have experienced one. Don't we want women to be fully informed before making such a life-altering decision? How many would, in fact, change their minds when they discover that it wasn't the quick fix they were hoping for?

Let me stop here and speak directly to the women who are reading this and have experienced one or more abortions. I implore you not to visit this site unless you are at a place in your healing where you can deal with the emotions that will surely surface. It is not a Christian site that offers a Christian solution; it would be far better for you to begin your road of healing by sharing your story with a strong and supportive Christian friend or mentor. It may even be necessary to see a Christian counselor, as I did years ago. The truth is, it will be difficult for you to talk to your daughter about what you have read above if you have not begun to process it for yourself. However, in the meantime let me caution you not to take your daughter to the afterabortion.com site if you suspect there may be the slightest possibility that she may have had an abortion.

While I believe the site serves a noble purpose, I also found it frustrating that much of the counsel is absent of any religious foundation. Instead the typical platitudes were offered such as, "The pain will lessen over time." "I know what you're feeling, and I wish I could help." "Have you tried talking to your boyfriend?" I mean, yikes, most of these girls need to ditch the boyfriend! The clear answer to their suffering and grief is the balm of healing that only Christ can offer. In the appendix, I include a poem that I wrote to my unborn child years ago as part of my journey of healing. You may or may not find it useful, but if given the opportunity, it is what I would want to tell each and every woman, both young and old, who is looking for comfort after the fact.

Babies Having Babies

While in the process of writing this chapter, the media is abuzz over a new report released by the U.S. Centers for Disease Control and Prevention stating that the nation's teen birth rate has risen for the first time in fourteen years. The birth rate had been dropping since 1991 until just recently when it jumped 3 percent from 2005 to 2006. In addition, the birth data for 2006 showed births to unmarried mothers has hit a new record high.[6] When the report released, predictably, there was finger pointing, and the general consensus was that abstinence-based sex education was to blame. Forget that a study in 2004 by the National Campaign to Prevent Teen Pregnancy found that 94 percent of teens want a strong message from society not to have sex, at least until they are out of high school.[7] Forget that teens are bombarded with a "just do it" message everywhere they look, and the encouragement to abstain is almost unheard of. Here are some fast facts regarding teen births:

> Ninety-five percent of teens want a strong message from society not to have sex, at least until they are out of high school.

- More than nine in ten teens who give birth keep their babies.[8]
- Nearly one in five teenagers who experience a premarital pregnancy will get pregnant again within a year.[9]
- Within two years, more than 31 percent will have a repeat pregnancy.[10]

- One in three teen mothers drops out of high school.[11]
- Three in ten teen mothers go on welfare within three years of the birth of their first child.[12]
- Of prison inmates between fifteen and nineteen years of age, 90 percent are products of an adolescent pregnancy.[13]

The Dangerous Glamorization of Single Motherhood

Amazingly, our girls today get a sugarcoated picture from Hollywood of out-of-wedlock pregnancies. In fact, within weeks of the news release regarding teen birthrates increasing for the first time in fourteen years, *Glamour* magazine responded by giving unwed mothers Bridget Moynahan and Spice Girl Melanie Brown a "Best of 2007" award "because they remained thrilled about their pregnancies even after their relationships fell apart." Margery Eagan, columnist for the *Boston Herald*, wrote a fabulous article entitled, "Single Mom's the Word," and noted that *Glamour* is "a distinctly influential bible to thousands of middle-class teenage girls." In her article she points out that *Glamour* has glamorized single motherhood by highlighting out-of-wedlock pregnancies such as Moynahan's and Brown's by singling them out as 2007's "Best Gutsy New Moms." The message is clear: "They're heroes. Role models of proud womanhood," she claims. Eagan further says, "cool" is exactly the message *Glamour* magazine is sending in its December cover story, a sort of trickle-down "isn't this swell!" intended for young women with neither the money, maturity, or skills of a Bridget Moynahan or a Melanie Brown.[14]

While I certainly commend these two women for having their babies when many would have opted for abortion, I hardly think we need to be handing them any awards. And before the hate mail starts to trickle in defending single moms, let me set the record straight: I am not criticizing the single moms whose husbands have bailed on them and the kids, leaving mom to pick up the pieces and be both mom and dad to the children. They have my utmost respect. What I'm suggesting is that if we're handing out awards to "Best Gutsy New Moms," let's recognize the young ladies who swam against the tide of the casual hook-up culture and somehow managed to remain pure for their wedding night. You know, the ones who did it in the right order: marriage first, then sex, then kids. (And yes, this may include women who, today, find themselves single.) Oh, but that's so old-fashioned! And besides, who needs fathers? They're so over-rated in the eyes of a sophisticated *Glamour* magazine.

While we're handing out the "gutsy mom" awards, how about highlighting moms who refuse "selective abortion" in a multiple-birth pregnancy when told it could endanger the lives of the other fetus(es)? Or how about those who refuse to abort when told they are carrying a baby with Down syndrome or a handicap and then devote their lives to loving and caring for these angels? Sounds pretty gutsy to me. Or what about the moms who open their hearts to children trapped in the foster care system, many of whom have special needs? Those would certainly be my personal picks if I were handing out "gutsy mom" awards.

Let's not fool ourselves here. *Glamour* would not be handing out a gutsy mom award to a teen girl who unexpectedly finds herself pregnant and decides to keep her baby. Even if she has two jobs and donates plasma to pay for diapers and formula, there will be no award. They may hand her a phone number to the local Planned Parenthood clinic, but she can forget about the "gutsy" label. I mean, seriously, what's so gutsy about a super rich celebrity who will, likely, lay down more money to decorate the baby's nursery than most of us did on our first home? Who do you think is going to change the dirty diapers and get up in the middle of the night when the baby has colic? My guess would be the gutsy *nanny*. What a strange world we live in. How ironic that the blame for the rise in teenage pregnancy will be attributed to the forces behind abstinence-based sex education while, in the meantime, the culture unashamedly peddles the glamorization of sex outside of marriage as the norm.

It only takes knowing one teen mother to know that the experience is anything but glamorous. Just ask the girls at Alley's House in Dallas, Texas (a haven for teen moms that is devoted to helping them through the crisis). Many of the girls claim their pregnancies were the result of growing up without a father in the picture and seeking out a strong male figure to fill the void. Unfortunately their "strong male figure" often turns out to be a wimp in the end. The girls claim that most of their boyfriends promised to stick around when told about the pregnancy but eventually bolted when they saw the reality involved in raising a child.[15] There's no nanny to help these girls with their babies. In fact, 46 percent of single mothers receive public assistance.[16]

Forty-six percent of single mothers receive public assistance.

I encourage you to be honest with your daughter about the difficulties. It will be a tricky balance because, on the one hand, we want to be clear that abortion is wrong and should not be considered as an option. On the other hand, we want to be completely honest about the difficulties that can come with being a teen mother, as well as those associated with putting a child up for adoption. The end goal, of course, is to leave them with a clear message that sex outside of marriage can lead to pregnancy, which in turn will leave them with less than ideal options. And regardless of which option is chosen, it will literally alter the course of their lives from that moment forward. In addition, we must make sure that our girls have not been brainwashed into thinking single motherhood is glamorous, noble, or chic at any age. While the Hollywood celebs make it look easy, we must continually remind our girls that they will not have access to a nanny or the money to lessen the blow.

While I certainly commend Jamie Lynn Spears and others like her who are in the media eye for choosing to have their babies in a culture that preaches abortion as a quick fix, I also fear that our girls are being left with the impression that it's "fun" and "trendy" to be a young mother with a baby on your hip. Our girls are not being exposed to a true picture of what goes on behind closed doors. Nanny or not, I can't imagine a single one of these celebrities who wouldn't welcome the presence of a loving husband and father for the times when the baby is up in the middle of the night with the croup or running a high fever. Let's make sure our girls are not absorbing this sugarcoated-single-motherhood-is-chic message.

CHAPTER ELEVEN

A Reality Check for Christian Parents

I have a friend who, when her kids were young, insisted on refer-ring to their private parts by the correct anatomical terms while I, on the other hand, provided my children with nicknames. She would tease me about it often and tell me that I was going to mess them up for life. My little nickname system worked just fine until one day when a new family moved into our neighborhood. I had heard that they also had a six-year-old boy, the same age as my oldest at the time, so we stopped by one day to introduce ourselves. When the mother introduced her son to my son, Ryan, I immedi-ately knew we had a problem. Unfortunately, he shared the same name as um, well, you know—I still can't say it! Anyway, I shot my son a pleading look to remain silent, but by the look on his face, I knew we would have plenty to talk about on the way home. I'll never forget his comment as we walked away: "Mom, why would anyone name their kid Willy?" Drats. I would have to come clean and just in time, mind you. The movie *Free Willy* released the following year. It's a good thing we cleared the matter up.

Just as I danced around the obvious for many years in an effort to avoid reality, many Christian parents today do the same thing when it comes to having the sex talk with their teens. However, if we are to be effective, we must address some real and present hurdles that are looming when it comes to talking to our kids candidly about sex outside of marriage.

Church Kids Are Having Sex, Too

Eighty percent of "evangelical" or "born again" teenagers think sex should be saved for marriage. Unfortunately, there appears to be a huge disconnect when it comes to walking the talk. According to a study, *Forbidden Fruit: Sex & Religion in the Lives of American Teenagers* by Mark Regnerus, a professor of sociology at the University of Texas at Austin, evangelical teens are actually more likely to have lost their virginity than either mainline Protestants or Catholics, and they lose their virginity at a slightly younger age— 16.3, as compared to 16.7 for mainline Protestants and Catholics. In addition, they are much more likely to have had three or more sexual partners by age seventeen (13.7 percent of evangelicals versus 8.9 percent for mainline Protestants).[1]

Equally disturbing, evangelical teens scored low on a quiz related to pregnancy and health risks. The authors of the study speculate that parents of "evangelical teens" may be talking to their kids about sex, but the conversation is more focused on the morals rather than the mechanics. In other words, we seem to have the "don't do it until your married" part down but stop short of giving them advice based on a hypothetical "but if you do decide to have sex. . . ." The articles further states, "Evangelical teens don't accept themselves as people who will have sex until they've already had it."[2]

Therein lies the problem. If they don't *expect* to have sex, they aren't *prepared* to have sex. And if we don't expect them to have sex, we don't leave them prepared should they succumb to the temptation and have sex. In fact, half of all mothers of sexually active teenagers mistakenly believe their children are still virgins, according to a team of researchers at the University of Minnesota Adolescent Health Center.[3]

Regnerus sums up our ignorance to the problem well. "For evangelicals, sex is a 'symbolic boundary' marking a good Christian from a bad one, but in reality, the kids are always 'sneaking across enemy lines.'"[4] That is a humbling thought for well-meaning Christian parents who can also relate to sneaking across enemy lines in their own teen years.

No doubt Christian parents are certainly in a quandary when it comes to having "the talk." On the one hand we want to make sure our teens are clear on the why behind God's mandate to save sex for marriage, but on the other hand, if we give them information beyond that, we fear it may convey permission to mess up. The study above found that abstinence pledgers are considerably less likely than nonpledgers to use birth control the first time they have sex because, as one girl told the researchers, "It just sort of happened."[5]

Speaking of virginity pledges, there is good news and bad news. Based on a study of more than twenty thousand young people who had taken virginity pledges in years prior, 88 percent admitted to have broken their pledge.[6] Obviously, that is bad news, especially

> Half of all mothers of sexually active teenagers mistakenly believe their children are still virgins.

if you were breathing a huge sigh of relief that your daughter has signed a pledge. The good news is that students who sign virginity pledges tend to postpone sexual activity by an average of eighteen months.[7]

Now I know what some of you are thinking. *What's so good about that if they are still giving into sex outside of marriage?* I concur with that thought and feel equally frustrated, yet every month we can buy is one extra month to equip them with information beyond that heartfelt pledge to God to wait until marriage. In addition, a study by The Heritage Foundation has found that "teens who make pledges have better life outcomes."[8] The study further found that pledgers are less likely to become pregnant (girls who are strong pledgers are more than 50 percent less likely to have a teen pregnancy than are nonpledgers) and less likely to give birth out of wedlock.

> Teens who make virginity pledges will also have fewer sexual partners and are far less likely to engage in sexual activity during the high school years.

Teens who make virginity pledges will also have fewer sexual partners and are far less likely to engage in sexual activity during the high school years.[9]

What is a mother to make of this information? When it gets right down to the nitty-gritty of the matter, what are we supposed to tell our daughters? While we are clearly not giving them enough information, how much is too much? In the remainder of this chapter, I will attempt to answer some of the above questions, as well as suggest a new and improved sex talk we can have with our daughters. Let me also offer the disclaimer that every child is different, and you, as the mother, will know best how to address this important topic with your daughter. My way is not necessarily the right way; it is merely a suggestion based on my background in ministering to preteen and teen girls and my knowledge of the climate of the current culture. Given the times, it is the conversation that I am personally having with my own daughter and, for that matter, my sons.

Many viewpoints exist among Christians regarding the most effective way to address sexual purity. It is oftentimes a heated topic that is fueled by much passion and good intent. That said, know that I am not an authority. I am a caring mother like you who wants what's best for my daughter—God's best. I run the same risk that every other Christian parent does. In the end, my daughter and/or sons could choose to reject the information I have given them and succumb to the temptation to have sex outside of marriage. While I hope that is not the case, I realize it is a real possibility. Therefore, know that I propose this new, upgraded sex talk in a spirit of humility.

No talk comes with a guarantee, but I can say this much: after having this conversation over the years with my own children, I can honestly say that I have done my part in impressing God's truth regarding sex upon my children. I will have taken advantage of teachable moments when we sit at home, walk along the road, lie down, and get up (see Deut. 6:7). Should they decide to forego God's plan for sex in spite of my teaching and instruction, I will not shrug my shoulders and say, "Where did I go wrong?" I will know I did all I could and continue to pray that their hearts would be sensitive and ripe to God's teaching, even if it's after the fact. Mothers, if we do our part on the front end, there is no need to sit around and wring our hands, wondering if they have given into or will give into the temptation.

The Challenge in Waiting

In the book *The Body Project*, author Joan Jacobs Brumberg states that "at the end of the last century, in the 1890s, a middle-class American girl was likely to menstruate at fifteen or sixteen and be a blushing virgin when she married in her early twenties. But by the 1900s, a girl of the same social class is likely to be sexually active before the age at which her great-great-grandmother had even begun to menstruate."[10]

Studies show that girls are developing earlier than ever before and with that early development come hormones. Couple that with the delay in marriage (the average age is twenty-six for women), and you see the challenge we face. A hundred years ago, remaining sexually pure until marriage, for the average girl, meant exercising self-control for four to six years. Today, for the average girl, delaying sex means exercising self-control for ten to fourteen years.

As Christian mothers, we often tell our girls to remain pure while at the same time we encourage them to delay marriage and enjoy being single. I will address attitudes regarding the popular mind-set that marriage should be delayed in the next conversation, but for the sake of this conversation, it is necessary to question whether this is an unrealistic expectation to place on our daughters. They can hardly escape the culture's girl-power message to climb the career ladder before considering marriage and motherhood, but are we also playing a part in making it difficult for our daughters to maintain their purity by peddling the same message? Seriously, no wonder 95 percent of women have sex before marriage! I can count on two hands the number of girls I know who made it to the altar with their virginity intact and who married prior to the age of twenty-six. Sadly, I don't even need one hand to count those who remained pure and married in their late twenties and thirties. Certainly, food for thought.

> A hundred years ago, remaining sexually pure until marriage, for the average girl, meant exercising self-control for four to six years. Today, for the average girl, delaying sex means exercising self-control for ten to fourteen years.

The Adolescent Brain: Act Now, Think Later

Another factor that needs to be considered before beginning "the talk" is the finding that for adolescents there is a lag between the body's capability and the mind's capacity to comprehend the consequences of sex.[11] Let me sum that up for you: When we tell our adolescent-aged daughters, "If you have sex before you're married, you could get pregnant," their brains are not cognitively developed enough to walk down a worst-case scenario path and consider the full weight of teen pregnancy. Their bodies are saying "do it," and their brains have not caught up to say, "If you do, you might get pregnant and find yourself up in the middle of the night with a colicky infant while your friends are at the senior prom." Nor are they able to see past the moment of desired pleasure to weigh the consequences of STDs, abortion, depression, tattered reputations, and the like.

This finding was especially helpful to me as I realized that I, personally, had somehow imagined that my daughter had the same picture in her mind that I did when I would caution her about the risks associated with out-of-wedlock sex. We have to help them walk the scenario down its path and paint a picture of the consequences for them rather than assume they have the cognitive ability to do so on their own. For example, when I shared with my daughter about my abortion, I went a step further than just offering a simple, "I really regret the abortion I had at the age of seventeen." I told her how bittersweet it was the first time I felt her brother move within my womb and realized what I had missed (and done). I told her that not a June goes by when I don't do the math to figure out how old that unborn child would be. Yes, I am forgiven, and I no longer feel shame, but at the same time I want my daughter to know the truth beyond a trite statement that "abortion is not a quick fix."

Another study related to the lag in cognitive development when it comes to adolescent reasoning concluded that "teenagers need 'practice at recognizing cues in the environment that signal possible danger before it's too late to act.'"[12] Therefore, it is critical to teach our daughters to recognize when they are in over their heads regarding sexual temptation. Stop for a minute and think about the biblical counsel we give them to "flee temptation." How often do we go a step further and give them practical ways to flee or the words to say when they find themselves in a precarious situation?

In my ministry to teen girls, I have encountered countless young women who say that they went too far sexually because they didn't know what to say in the situation. Again, this may sound absurd to those of us who are adults and are better equipped to put our thoughts into words, but for an adolescent teen with raging hormones and little ability to think on her feet, it's a real and present problem. For example, when discussing this with my own daughter, I have encouraged her to come up with actual verbiage of what she might say when faced with a sexually tempting situation and, as ridiculous as it may sound, practice her lines in front of her bathroom mirror to get them down pat.

Valerie F. Reyna, professor of human development and psychology at the New York State College of Human Ecology at Cornell and an author of the study, also cautions:

> Younger adolescents don't learn from consequences as
> well as older adolescents do. So rather than relying on
> them to make reasoned choices or to learn from the
> school of hard knocks, a better approach is to supervise
> them. . . . A young teenage girl should not be left alone
> in the house with her boyfriend, and responsible adults
> should be omnipresent and alcohol absent when teenagers
> have parties.[13]

In summary, parents should draw firm boundaries and behave like parents. If our kids are unable to assess all the risks associated with an action, we essentially step in and protect them from themselves. One of my son's college-aged friends shared candidly with me that he had ended a relationship with his Christian girlfriend of more than three years in an effort to maintain sexual purity after having gone too far in the relationship. He mentioned that part of their temptation was a lack of rules or boundaries on the part of her parents when he was at her home. Mind you, these are Christian parents. He shared that even while dating in high school, it was not uncommon to be left alone in the house while her parents were gone. In other words, he was stunned and amazed that her parents trusted them as much as they did! He ended his comments with the conclusion, "When I have kids . . . !"

> **I**f our kids are unable to assess all the risks associated with an action, we essentially step in and protect them from themselves.

What can we learn from this information regarding the lag in cognitive development? Dr. Reyna stated that as people grow older and more experienced, they became more intuitive, and more of their decisions are based on what she calls "gist," an overall sense of what is the best course of action. And who better than Mother to help guide our kids to the best course of action and teach them to look to God for "intuition," all the while, providing plenty of rules and supervision along the way.

CHAPTER TWELVE

A New and Improved Sex Talk

I will never forget the night I was tucking Paige into bed and she asked for the first time, "Mom, where do babies come from?" She was ten years old and in the fifth grade. Old enough, I thought, to handle the truth. I told her that "sex is a beautiful act to be enjoyed by husband and wife in marriage" and then proceeded to launch into the mechanics of sex. Before I ever had a chance to finish, she held her hand in the air and yelled, "Stop! That is the absolute grossest thing I have ever heard. Please tell me you and Daddy have never done that!" In hindsight, maybe it would have gone over better had I used the term "Willy" instead of that anatomically correct *p* word.

Maybe you have a similar story. The sex talk has never been easy or comfortable, but it is necessary if we are to raise healthy, well-adjusted children. Where do we begin? What do we say? How much do we share? This chapter will help answer those questions.

The Best Sex-Ed Teacher Your Daughter Will Have Is YOU

When talking to our daughters about sexual purity, we could easily give up and declare defeat. Trust me, plenty of parents have. I am always amazed by the focus many parents place on academics and/or extracurricular activities and the lack of concern over integrity, virtue, and moral character. Mom and Dad will take off work to shuttle their daughters all over town (and out of town) for school or club sports, but when it comes to setting their alarms for church, forget it. That's the only day to sleep in, for heaven's sake! (Or so we're told.) And from what I can tell, the problem is just as bad among Christians. Parents are pooped out from pouring their energy into things that won't matter for eternity and left with little time to disciple their kids. It's no surprise that most Christian kids are behaving just like the rest of the world.

Most of us are claiming Proverbs 22:6, "Train a child in the way he should go, and when he is old he will not turn from it," but the truth is, little training is going on.

> Parents are pooped out from pouring their energy into things that won't matter for eternity and left with little time to disciple their kids.

When teaching our daughters "the way she should go" regarding sex, many moms feel like it's a lost cause given the climate of the culture and the high number of kids (including Christian kids) who give in. You're not likely to fall in that category, or you wouldn't have picked up this book. However, I'm sure we can all think of parents who are standing on the sidelines and scratching their heads, oblivious to what's shaking down around them. And then there are the parents who make excuses, discounting the problem with stupid clichés like, "Kids will be kids," and "You're only young once."

Study after study confirms that there is a direct link between engaged, caring parents and children making wise choices. Don't ever doubt the power you have in influencing your daughter when it comes to sexual purity. One study indicated that teenagers in grades eight through eleven who perceive that their mother disapproves of them engaging in sexual intercourse are more likely than their peers to delay sexual activity.[1]

The National Campaign to Prevent Teen Pregnancy conducted a survey that questioned one thousand young people ages twelve to nineteen and 1,008 adults age twenty and older and found that 45 percent of teens said their parents most influence their decisions about sex compared to 31 percent who said their friends are most influential. Religious leaders were only the most influential among 7 percent, while teachers and sex educators stood at 6 percent and the media at 4 percent.[2] Given this news flash, let's take a look at four factors that will greatly increase the odds that your daughters will be committed (or recommitted) to sexual purity.

The Must-Have List for Sexual Purity

1. Open Lines of Communication

A key factor in raising daughters who desire sexual purity is to talk about it. A good rule of thumb to remember when it comes to discussing sex is to keep the conversation simple and keep it going. The first step is making sure your daughter has a grasp of what the purpose of sex is and what God has to say about it. It doesn't have to be complicated, and, in fact, it needs to be simple enough for a youngster to grasp, as many will begin asking questions about sex in grade school. I love the approach that sexual abstinence expert

Pam Stenzel takes in her book *Sex Has a Price Tag: Discussions about Sexuality, Spirituality, and Self-Respect*. Here it is in a nutshell:

1. Humans did not create sex, God did.

2. Since God created sex, He's the one who understands it the best.

3. Since God understands sex better than anyone, a person who wants to have great sex (and why would anyone want to have rotten sex?) needs to know what God says about sex.

What does God have to say about sex? Sex was created for one, and only one, situation—marriage.[3]

Once they are clear on the basics regarding the purpose of sex and God's view of sex, then you can begin to incorporate some of the information we have discussed into your conversations, assuming, of course, she is old enough. Break down the information into bite-size conversations rather than dumping an entire chapter's worth of information on her at one time. Build stories around the statistics we have addressed in order to bring them to life.

Your daughter should have a good grasp on what the culture is *not* telling her about sex before she enters her sophomore year in high school. If she is older than that right now, begin right away! (**Note:** Depending on her level of understanding and maturity, she may need to hear this information in middle school.) Continue the conversations over the years, taking advantage of teachable moments as they occur. For example, when the news hit about Jamie Lynn Spears's (Britney Spears's sister) pregnancy at sixteen, I took the opportunity to talk about it with my daughter. In addition to talking about obvious consequences such as the loss of her career, childhood, and reputation, I also took the opportunity to commend her for keeping the baby when many girls, had they been in her shoes, would have raced to the nearest abortion clinic in an effort to "take care of the problem" so they could continue their ascent up the Hollywood ladder. Don't let these opportunities pass by.

When talking to your daughter, provide opportunities for two-way communication. One survey found that 88 percent of teens said it would be easier to postpone sexual activity and avoid teen pregnancy if they were able to have more open, honest conversations about sex with their parents. Interestingly, the same study found that only 32 percent of adults surveyed believe parents are most influential in their teens' decisions about sex.[4]

> Eighty-eight percent of teens said it would be easier to postpone sexual activity and avoid teen pregnancy if they were able to have more open, honest conversations about sex with their parents.

2. Relationship

One study found that teenagers who "feel highly connected to their parents and report that their parents are warm, caring and supportive—are far more likely to delay sexual activity than their peers."[5] Another unrelated study found that close relationships with mothers seemed to discourage youngsters from sexual activity. However, I should note that it also found that the effect diminished with age and, among girls, disappeared altogether. Author of the study, Barbara Huberman notes, "High levels of mother-teen connectedness were not significantly associated with delays in sexual intercourse among 10th-11th-grade girls." She offered the explanation that "girls in their late teens generally felt a powerful need to claim their independence, in part by defying their mothers."[6]

All the more reason, moms, to establish the relationship early on and begin the conversations when the time is right. If (or when) the relationship becomes tenuous, we can rest in the knowledge that we have provided them with the facts along the way. And while I concur with Ms. Huberman's assessment that "girls in their late teens generally felt a powerful need to claim their independence," I'm not so sure I agree with her conclusion that many girls will do it for the sheer sake of "defying their mothers." The relationship doesn't have to be fractured during these years, just different. It's important that we don't allow our daughters to push us away in these years and that we fight to keep the lines of communication open. I mentioned in chapter 7 that my daughter and I have a standing date every couple of weeks where just the two of us go to dinner. While broaching some topics was somewhat awkward initially, I found that her willingness to open up increased over time. Now that she is away at college, hopefully she will remember not only the topics we discussed, but the relationship we developed along the way. Even though we won't be able to meet every couple of weeks, I'm only a phone call away.

3. Boundaries/Supervision

When talking to our daughters about sex, Sarah Brown, director of the National Campaign to Prevent Teen Pregnancy, said that talk alone is insufficient. She further stated that what matters even more, especially among younger teenagers, is a relationship in which parents keep close tabs on them, knowing who their friends are and what they do together. Amazing. Imagine that—deep down inside, our children feel more loved and cared for when they have boundaries and supervision. They want their parents to be parents, not their buddies. Brown concluded that the ideal home for fostering this kind of closeness is one open to friends of the children. She said, "When a house is open to young people, there is this sense they can be themselves. There's food, space, caring adults around."[7]

When my oldest son entered high school, we added a game room onto the back of our house and declared, "This is the hangout. Your friends are welcome here." It's been six years and now my youngest is in high school. I could write a whole book on the benefits of that game room. Over the years we have come to love our children's friends as if they were our own. Many will come over and visit my husband and me even when our kids are not home. Some of these kids are not believers, and I pray for opportunities to share the love of Christ with them. God has answered that prayer over and over again. More importantly, we have provided our children with a place to gather with their friends, all the while under the safe supervision of caring adults in the next room. You don't have to take out a loan and build a game room. I have heard of others converting garages into an extra space or using their living rooms. All you need is one spare room and an open heart. We don't forbid our children to go to other people's homes, but we have at times required that their friends come to our house first so we can get to know them.

4. Faith

A survey that studied evangelical teens found that 88 percent of those making virginity pledges will end up breaking them. One group in particular stood out when it comes to success: the 16 percent of American teens who describe religion as "extremely important" in their lives. In other words, the radical believers who aren't afraid to walk their talk and are more concerned with pleasing God than pleasing others. The study found that when these teens pledge, they mean it. The study further found that the ideal conditions are a "group of pledgers who form a self-conscious minority that perceives itself as special, even embattled."[8]

The 5 Percent Factor

For some reason the word *special* jumped off the page when I first read it and immediately got my attention. What if parents, rather than conveniently ignore the depressing statistics regarding the percentage of people who will have sex before marriage (approximately 95 percent) when discussing sex with their children, decided instead to come clean. Rather than imply that "all Christian kids know that sex should be saved for marriage" and assume that most will live up to that standard (when in fact, most won't), what if the conversation sounded more like this:

"You know honey, the truth is that 95 percent of people will have sex outside of marriage. Most of your Christian friends will give into the temptation to have sex and experience less than God's best. Only 5 percent will make it to their wedding day with their purity intact and experience sex exactly as God intended. Only 5 percent will receive this special blessing. Only 5 percent will be absolutely free from worry of STDs and worry over out-of-wedlock pregnancies and the trauma that comes with decisions such as abortion and putting a baby up for adoption. Only 5 percent will be spared from depression, guilt, and shame that are common among those who are promiscuous. Only 5 percent will be among those who have a decreased likelihood of divorce and greater odds of a happy marriage and family life. Only 5 percent will have succeeded in practicing self-restraint when it comes to having sex outside of marriage and will, no doubt, stand a greater chance of practicing self-restraint when it comes to sexual temptations within marriage. Should you marry someone who is also fortunate enough to be among this special group of 5 percent, you will also have a greater peace of mind that your spouse will be more likely to practice self-restraint from sexual temptations within marriage and will not stray. Finally, only 5 percent will experience the fullness of what God meant when He said 'the two will become one.' Only 5 percent will become one . . . with only one. What do you think? Do you want to be among this special group of 5 percent, or do you want to join the other 95 percent who insisted on setting the ground rules for sex and ignoring God in the process?"

Wow, it makes me wish I had been among this special group of 5 percent who honored God with their bodies. Author Pam Stenzel tells a story in her book of a college student who committed to wait to have sex until marriage. "He's the only guy on his football team who's still a virgin. He asked an older man what he could say to his friends when they ridiculed him or mocked his decision. The man said, 'Tell them you can become just like them any time you want, but they can never again be like you. That's far more valuable than anything they've ever experienced.'"[9]

CHAPTER THIRTEEN

Additional Conversations

Most Christian parents feel like they're ahead of the curve if they can manage to deliver the standard sex talk to their child at least once before they walk across the stage at graduation. And often that talk boils down to a basic message of "don't do it until you're married because God says to wait." Because it is limited in scope, it fails to recognize that other necessary conversations need to be covered if we are to give our children a more comprehensive view of sex education. This chapter will detail other critical conversations to consider having with your daughter.

How Much Should You Share about Your Past?

This is perhaps the most common question I receive from mothers when I speak at conferences. Most of us, truth be told, made plenty of mistakes along the way and wrestle with how much information, if any, we should share with our daughters. Here are some general rules when it comes to sharing:

- Never share details with your daughter related to the number of guys you may have slept with or specific details about what you did. Doing so does not serve a purpose and falls under the category of TMI (too much information). For example, I shared with my daughter, "I was not a virgin when I married, and I regret my decision not to wait." The focus should be the *regret* rather than the act itself.
- Never share information regarding your past with your daughter if she is younger than middle school. Depending on the maturity and temperament of your daughter, she may not be ready for it in middle school. If she is somewhat sheltered and not even displaying an interest in boys, what is the purpose? We want to be preventive, yet at the same time be sensitive not to rob them of their innocence. Whether you are sharing your own regret or the regret of others you knew that gave in, pray and ask God to nudge your heart when the time is right.
- Never share information with your daughter about experiences where you have yet to experience healing. Our daughters are not equipped to help us process guilt and shame over our past actions. When we share, we must, ourselves, be walking in victory. I am talking about particularly traumatic events we may have experienced as a result of poor choices (extreme promiscuity, the contraction of an STD, an abortion, giving a child up for adoption, alcohol or drug abuse that led to unwanted sex). Such accounts can be valuable to share with our daughters when the time is right; however, we must be at

a place in our healing where our motive is to provide our
daughters with an example of sincere regret rather than to
lean on them for comfort. God has forgiven your sin "as
far as the east is from the west" (Ps. 103:12). If you have
not embraced that truth, share your pain instead with a
trusted Christian friend or counselor who can encourage
you in the road to healing. Also, be careful not to share
too much information. For example, what purpose does it
serve to share that you have had more than one abortion
or that your abortion was in the second trimester? Again,
remember that the focus is on the regret rather than the
details. When the time was right, I shared the poem
I wrote to my unborn child with each of my children. It
offered a good balance of regret while at the same time
it emphasized God's healing and forgiveness.

Refrain from sharing information related to past sexual
abuse with your children. Perhaps they may be ready in
their adult years to hear such information, but what is the
purpose of telling them this information (unless, of course,
they have been abused). A dear friend of mine regrets
telling her children this information as they struggled
for years with how to process what they had been told.
Some issues of our past are better left to a trusted
Christian mentor, friend, or perhaps even a Christian
counselor.

Never share information regarding someone else's past in
an effort to gain a teachable moment with your daughter
unless you have their prior permission. "So-and-so at
church had several abortions and shared in our small
group Bible study." No! "I have a dear friend . . ." would
be a better approach but never give names without prior
consent. This also goes for girls your daughter's age about

whom you may have heard a buzz. Gossip is never justified even if it's intended to be a teachable moment.

Most of us, truth be told, are hesitant to some degree to share our own past regret because we fear that our daughters may walk away with the impression that if "Mom messed up, I can mess up, too." I can't guarantee you that they won't. If your daughter is currently in a rebellious phase and looking for permission to misbehave, she may draw that conclusion. However, if you convey a heartfelt sense of regret mixed with a sincere intent to spare your own daughter from making the same mistakes, I doubt she will race out to repeat your same sin.

> Never share information regarding someone else's past in an effort to gain a teachable moment with your daughter unless you have their prior permission.

Preparing Your Daughter for Her Honeymoon

Several years back one of my young coworkers who was just weeks away from her wedding shared with me that she was afraid to have sex and not sure what to expect. She was raised in a Christian home and attended a private Christian school, and she confessed that her mother had never once broached the topic of sex. Mothers, she is not alone. Over the years of serving in ministry to girls, I have heard from others who express a similar fear over what to expect on the honeymoon night. While I have yet to speak candidly with my daughter regarding first-time sex, I plan to do so long before her honeymoon night. We have no shortage of resources to help us in this pursuit, many of which can be found online if we find ourselves in need of a refresher course.

I feel I also need to mention a handful of Christian girls I have counseled at past events who were virgins when they married and now struggle with *liking* sex after hearing "don't do it" for so long. In other words, once it was permissible, they had a hard time separating themselves from the "sex is wrong" message. Mothers, we must make absolutely sure that our daughters know that sex is a wonderful blessing from God and that He created it not only for procreation purposes but also for pleasure. I hope I have sufficiently conveyed to my daughter that sex is not a chore or duty but, in fact, a wonderful gift from God to be enjoyed in marriage. And while we're at it, let's make sure our girls know that being sensual and sexy is OK in the marriage bedroom. While our culture has blasted our girls with the encouragement to cultivate their sensualities, the Christian community has worked hard to counter that message (and rightly so). However, we need to make sure that we have not left our daughters with the general message that sexiness and sensuality are altogether evil and have no place in a Christian marriage. Who among us doesn't desire for our husbands to find us sensual and sexy? Better yet, who among us (that is married) doesn't have a husband who desires for his wife to be sensual and sexy?

If You Suspect Your Daughter Has Already Had Sex

Maybe as you are reading this, you suspect that your daughter has already had sex and you're left wondering where to go from here. Certainly, you don't give up that battle and declare defeat. The evidence presented reminds us that there is great benefit to committing to secondary virginity as well as support for the number of sexual partners influencing the future of marriage and happiness. It could be that your daughter is having sex, but she desires to change. (Remember, statistics show that nearly two-thirds of girls regret their decision to have sex and wish they had waited.) In this situation I would highly recommend that you meet with her on a weekly basis to discuss much of what we have learned thus far. Draw boundaries and supervise your daughter. Be picky about who she dates (if she's allowed to date) and let her know that the lines of communication are open. Most importantly, remind her that she is forgiven of her sin and that God's best for her from this point forward is secondary virginity. There is no need to beat her over the head with her sin and shame her. That's not God's way, and it shouldn't be our way either. Romans 8:1 reminds us, "There is no condemnation for those who belong to Christ Jesus."

On the other hand, if after discussing the matter with your daughter, you discover that she is unrepentant, it is most likely because (1) she doesn't want to risk losing her boyfriend or (2) she has wandered from the path of God and is callous to His truth regarding sex outside of marriage. Regardless, you must open up the lines of communication in an effort to begin conversations about the information we have discussed. I would begin by praying for the right time and setting to approach your daughter. Ask God to do a mighty work on her heart in advance. Prayer will be your most powerful force. You cannot sway her heart, but God can.

When talking to her, emphasize that your motive is concern, love, and her future well-being. This is a tricky dance, especially if you've come to the conclusion that she should no longer see this young man while she lives under your roof. If that is a boundary you need to draw, I encourage you to draw it while, at the same time, reminding her that your motive is love. Yes, there is always the risk that she will enter into an all-out rebellion and continue down her wayward path. The sobering truth is that, if she wants to find a way to continue having sex with her boyfriend (or hooking up), she will find a way, even while living under your roof. At this point, if you suspect that she is planning to continue in sin, you are caught in a precarious position. The question then becomes, do you or do you not encourage her to practice birth control? If I were personally facing this situation with my own daughter and she was clearly not broken over her sin or willing to repent, I would continue to focus on God's standard and not deviate one iota. God's Word reminds us of the standard: "Be holy, because I am holy" (1 Pet. 1:16). I would certainly not sit her down and go over a list of birth control options because to do so in a sense, says, "Hey, God's word says to 'be holy,' but since you insist on being 'less than holy,' might I suggest a plan B to help you cut your losses?" I could not say or do something that in good conscience would further contribute to her sin.

I know this sounds like a stern brand of tough love, but consider this comment from a young lady who wrote to popular radio host, Dr. Laura (Schlesinger):

> I grew up with parents who had a zero tolerance policy for sexual activity outside of marriage. Sure, when I was a child our conversations about sex were calm and relaxed. We talked openly about the consequences and reasons to wait. However, when I became a teenager I knew that if I had sex and got pregnant, I was on my own. I knew that if I had sex they would not pay for college. I knew that if I had sex there were not only going to be consequences with my parents . . . and you know what? As a teenager, losing the love and respect of my parents was enough of a consequence for me to abstain when my friends were not. Parents need to be stern about sex outside of marriage— not compassionate. If my parents had told me in advance that I could come to them after I had sex and all I would receive was a big hug and a trip to the drug store, I would have had no reason to abstain.[1]

Sex Education through the Years

Believe it or not, sex education begins at an early age. I found some wonderful tips from the Mayo Clinic offered on their site. They break it down according to age and level of understanding.[2]

Ages Eighteen Months to Three Years

Children begin to learn about their own bodies. Teach your child the proper names for sex organs. Otherwise, he or she might get the idea that something is wrong with these parts of the body.

Ages Three to Four

Take advantage of everyday opportunities to discuss sex. If there's a pregnancy in the family, for example, tell your children that babies grow in a special place inside the mother. If your children want more details on how the baby got there or how the baby will be born, offer them.

Consider these examples:

- How do babies get inside a mommy's tummy? You might say: "A mom and a dad make a baby by holding each other in a special way."
- How are babies born? For some kids, it might be enough to say, "Doctors and nurses help babies who are ready to be born."
- Where do babies come from? Try to give a simple and direct response, such as: "Babies grow in a special place inside the mother." As your child matures, you can add more details.

Teach your child that the parts of the body covered by a bathing suit are private and that no one should be allowed to touch them without permission.

Ages Five to Seven

Questions about sex will become more complex as your child tries to understand the connection between sexuality and making babies. He or she may turn to friends for some of these answers. Because children can pick up faulty information about sex and reproduction, it may be best to ask what your child knows about a particular topic before you start explaining it.

Ages Eight to Twelve

Children between the ages of eight and twelve worry a lot about whether they are "normal." Children of the same age mature at wildly different rates. Reassure your child that he or she is well within the normal range of development.

Ages Thirteen and Above

The American Academy of Pediatrics recommends that before they reach puberty children should have a basic understanding of:

- The names and functions of male and female sex organs
- What happens during puberty and what the physical changes of puberty mean—movement into young womanhood or young manhood
- The nature and purpose of the menstrual cycle
- What sexual intercourse is and how females become pregnant
- How to prevent pregnancy
- Same-sex relationships
- Masturbation
- Activities that spread sexually transmitted diseases (STDs), in particular AIDS
- Your expectations and values[3]

Be honest, open, and matter-of-fact.

Talking about sexual matters with your child can make you both feel uncomfortable and embarrassed. Let your child guide the talk with his or her questions. Don't giggle or laugh, even if the question is cute. Try not to appear overly embarrassed or serious.

If you have been open with your child's questions since the beginning, your child will more likely come to you with his or her questions in the future. The best place for your child to learn about relationships, love, commitment, and respect is from you.[4]

It's *OK* to Dream about Marriage and Motherhood!

CHAPTER FOURTEEN

The Anti-marriage Agenda

My daughter logged countless hours in her toddler and early elementary years playing dress-up. Her favorite getup by far was a pretend wedding dress that came complete with a veil, white gloves, wedding ring, and a pair of desperately uncomfortable plastic slip-on heels that were at two times the length of her tiny feet. Afraid she might turn her ankle while trying to shuffle her way down the pretend aisle to say her wedding vows, I once suggested she trade the shoes for her white, padded ballerina slippers.

"Mom," she snapped with the sarcasm of a teenager, "brides don't wear slippers on their wedding day! Did you wear slippers on your wedding day?"

"Well," I stammered, "Come to think of it, no. I wore desperately uncomfortable slip-on heels, so you make a good point. Carry on, my little bride."

Growing up in the same church for all of her years, half the boys in the youth group were forced to play the part of the unwilling groom in their younger years. One boy swears his first kiss was a peck on Paige Courtney's cheek at the tender age of four at the end of one of her pretend wedding ceremonies. He came over to play one afternoon and was promptly issued a blue blazer from Paige's brother's closet and ordered to wait for her at the bottom of the stairs. The way he tells the story, the kiss was a result of Paige's threat made through clenched teeth, "If you don't kiss me, I will never, ever, play with you again." Sigh. That's my girl. Her dress-up years are long behind her, but the dream of being a bride still remains. Hopefully, she won't have to issue the same threat to her beloved groom while standing at the altar on her real wedding day.

My husband and I did nothing to instill this bridal fantasy. It was as if she was born wired to wed, and until the moment arrived, there was plenty of time to practice for the big day. She and her friends would stage countless mock weddings and march their Barbies down a pretend aisle to meet their anxious Kens. Unfortunately, the anti-marriage forces present in culture today would do their best to kill the dream of marriage for our girls and replace their innocent hums of "dum-dum-de-dum" into chants of "dumb-dumb-de-dumb." Their message is clear: marriage stifles independence and threatens the "girl power" message that our girls have been force-fed since birth.

The current attitude about marriage can be summed up by a Yoplait yogurt commercial I saw on TV. Two women—perhaps in their mid to late twenties, dressed in their bridesmaids' gowns, and kicked back at a table during the reception—joke with each other while savoring their yogurt one spoonful at a time.

"This is like 'burning this dress' good; 'getting these shoes off good'; 'getting put with an usher who's not shorter than you good.'" An announcer chimes in on cue: "Rich, creamy Yoplait yogurt; it is so good" to which one of the girls tops it off with a confident, "Not catching the bouquet good." They raise their yogurt cups for a celebratory toast and toss their heads back in laughter. The message is clear: better to be *them*—single, independent, and self-focused, rather than *the bride*—their poor sap of a friend who took the marital plunge and, no doubt, forfeited any hope of future happiness.

Fifty years ago fashion magazines geared to young women (including *Seventeen*) were littered with ads for sterling silver flat-ware, china, engagement rings, and Lane hope chests. The average age of marriage for young women in 1950 was twenty, so marriage was certainly on the mind and heart of the average young lady. Not far off in the future, it was on their radars even if they weren't yet dating a viable candidate. Any reference to marriage in today's fashion magazines is a stern warning to avoid it like the plague. *Elle* magazine's expert on relationships advised a woman who wanted to get married that she should marry her dog instead because he's "the only creature who will love you more than you love yourself." *Cosmo* tells women who are "dying to get married" that they need to try to "enjoy dating more."[1]

> Any reference to marriage in today's fashion magazines is a stern warning to avoid it like the plague.

From fashion magazines to shows like *Friends, Sex in the City, Grey's Anatomy,* and the like, the message is clear: enjoy being single. No need to be tied down when you can get all the sex you want with as many men as you want without any commitment required. And God forbid that any of our girls say they are looking forward to becoming wives and mothers! They will likely be met with pitying stares that imply they lack common sense or the smarts to make it on their own.

Anyone who minimizes the effect our culture has had on influencing marriage attitudes needs to check out the latest census statistics. Consider this: in 1965 nearly 90 percent of women ages twenty-five to twenty-nine were married.[2] Compare that to today where almost three-quarters of men and almost two-thirds of women in their twenties in 2006 said they had never been married.[3] The last six years alone have shown a drastic increase with 73 percent of men ages twenty to twenty-nine, claiming they had never been married in 2006 as compared to 64 percent in 2000. For women, 62.2 percent had never been married in 2006, as compared to 53.4 percent in 2000.[4] In other words, fifty years ago, if you weren't married in your twenties, you were in a small 10 percent minority. Today those who marry in their twenties are in the minority (32 percent). What is going on here?

Let the Brainwashing Begin

Lest you doubt that the media has some biased views on marriage, consider the celebratory headlines in January 2007 over the breaking news regarding the census data finding that the majority of American women are unmarried for the first time in history. One metro daily explains, "Who needs a man? Not most women." MSNBC warns, "Watch out, men! More women opt to live alone." CBS says, "More Women Saying 'I Don't.'" One syndicated newspaper cartoon depicts a happily divorced woman remembering her ex-husband bellowing, "Where's my dinner?! Iron my shirts!! Lose weight!!!" Several others depict women pondering the single life as their fat, lazy husbands drink beer and watch the game. One female blogger summed up the female blogosphere's reaction: "Hurray for

All Single Women! You Go Girls!"[5] *The New York Times* heralded the message with the enthusiasm of a lottery win.[6]

Clearly our young people are buying the message. A study by the National Marriage Project of not-yet-married heterosexual men and women in their twenties found that women are just as committed as men to making it on their own and getting a place of their own before marriage. Compared to their male peers, these noncollege women are even more fiercely determined "to take care of myself."[7] It further found that the mating culture for today's twenty-somethings is not oriented to marriage, as it has been in times past, nor is it dedicated to romantic love. Based on the reports of these noncollege singles, it is perhaps best described as a culture of sex without strings and relationships without rings.[8]

Another study that examined twenty recently published undergraduate marriage and family textbooks commonly used on college campuses found that the textbooks "repeatedly suggest that marriage is more of a problem than a solution."[9] They further found a theme in the general message that marriage can hold "special dangers, particularly for women who, if they don't find marriage physically threatening, will likely find it psychologically stifling."[10] The potential downside of marriage often receives exaggerated treatment while the benefits of marriage are frequently downplayed or all together ignored.[11]

Danielle Crittenden, author of the book *What Our Mothers Didn't Tell Us*, notes that "the modern fairy tale ending is the reverse of the traditional one: A woman does not wait for Prince Charming to bring her happiness; she lives happily ever after only by refusing to wait for him—or by actually rejecting him."[12] In 1970, the median age of first marriage for women was just under twenty-one. Today the median age at first marriage has risen to just short of twenty-six.[13] While the gain of five years may not sound alarming at first glance, keep in mind that the number continues to rise, putting many young women into the danger zone as fertility continues to decline. Unfortunately, little can be done to slow the biological clock and extend the years of fertility in direct proportion to this increase. Almost everywhere we turn another Hollywood personality is pushing forty and a baby stroller at the same time. Of course, rarely do we hear of the price they paid to address any infertility hurdles they encountered along the way. Hurdles, mind you, they are better able to afford. Yet we continue to hear the message, "What's the hurry? Enjoy being single! You have many years ahead of you for marriage and motherhood. It's all about you, you, you!" I wonder how many women have discovered the hard way that life can be rather lonely when you enter your thirties and all you have is you, you, you.

Hurry Up and Wait

I have a young friend who upon graduating from college several years ago boldly stated: "Marriage is not even something I think about. It's the furthest thing from my mind. I won't give it a moment's thought until I've built my career and have been on my own for awhile—you know, maybe in my thirties." My young friend just celebrated her twenty-fifth birthday and confessed to me recently that she is beginning to think about marriage, much to her own shock. Without a candidate in sight, she expressed worry that as birthdays continue to come on schedule, the spouse and kids may not. What happened to being in her thirties? I thought that was her "planned" schedule.

Many of our girls are buying the lie that marriage and motherhood can be postponed indefinitely.

Many of our girls are buying the lie that marriage and motherhood can be postponed indefinitely. The culture has shouted, "You can have it all!" and they actually believed it. Like ordering fast food from a drive-through, marriage and motherhood are life events you choose on your timetable and your terms when you have a sudden hunger pang for it. Unfortunately, by the time many girls pull through the drive-through with their stomachs growling in their late twenties and early thirties, they discover that what they long for is no longer being offered on the menu. Then they look up and notice the young mothers ordering Happy Meals and corralling their little ones in the play area. They used to pity them for trading their valuable single years of independence to change dirty diapers and wipe snotty noses. Strangely, now they begin to wonder what it's like to be them. Oh, many will in fact marry. No one tells the other part of the story when it comes to delayed marriage. We hear nothing about the difficulties that arise when adjusting to marriage after years spent single and unencumbered. We hear nothing about the impact the number of sexual partners has on the health of a marriage on down the road. We hear nothing about the heartache that arises when problems of infertility surface. And we hear nothing about the exhaustion that comes from raising little ones in the years our own parents were gearing up for retirement.

And then there are the dear Christian girls who want nothing more than to be married and start a family in their twenties, but find themselves in their thirties and forties single and/or childless, unwilling victims of the delayed marriage trend. Our churches are bursting at the seams with this fast-growing segment of the population and scrambling to minister to their unique needs. These young ladies are doing the math, and they are panicked. Listening to these unmarried women in their early to mid-thirties as they express disappointment over their still-single status fuels my passion to address the topic in this book as a necessary conversation we must have with our own daughters. As I hear their plight and ponder the catch-22 that entraps them, it dawns on me that my daughter could someday be in their shoes. These beautiful, virtuous, on-fire-for-God women can't even recall the last time someone asked them out on a date.

The Real Winners

The Christian guys their age can hardly be described as "panicked." And why should they be? They are financially stable, have no biological clock ticking away, and virtually no external pressures to wed. They have their pick of a sea of women (both young and not so young) who are bidding for their attention.

A special essay on young, not-yet-married men's attitudes on the timing of marriage found that men in the study expressed a desire to marry and have children sometime in their lives but were in no hurry. They enjoy their single lives and experience few of the traditional pressures from church, employers, or the society that once encouraged men to marry. Moreover, the sexual revolution and the trend toward cohabitation offer men some of the benefits of marriage without its obligations.[14]

> Moreover, the sexual revolution and the trend toward cohabitation offer men some of the benefits of marriage without its obligations.

If there was ever proof that our young women are the real losers when it comes to this so-called "freedom" peddled by the sexual revolution and women's liberation proponents in the 1960s and 1970s, it is revealed in the study's list of "Ten Reasons Why Men Won't Commit." Get ready to grumble:

1. They can get sex without marriage more easily than in times past.
2. They can enjoy the benefits of having a wife by cohabiting rather than marrying (Translation: SEX!).

3. They want to avoid divorce and its financial risks.

4. They want to wait until they are older to have children.

5. They fear that marriage will require too many changes and compromises.

6. They are waiting for the perfect soul mate, and she hasn't yet appeared.

7. They face few social pressures to marry.

8. They are reluctant to marry a woman who already has children.

9. They want to own a house before they get a wife.

10. They want to enjoy single life as long as they can.[15]

The study concludes, "If this trend continues, it will not be good news for the many young women who hope to marry and bear children before they begin to face problems associated with declining fertility."[16]

Is it any wonder that the number of unmarried women between the ages of thirty and thirty-four has more than tripled during the past thirty years and that the percentage of childless women in their early forties has doubled?[17] Wendy Shalit, author of the book *Girls Gone Mild*, describes this cruel irony:

Single women approaching their late twenties become
more serious about the search for a marriage partner.
They've gained confidence in their capacity to "make it on
their own," and they are ready to think about marriage.
However, many say the "men aren't there," they're "not
on the same page," or they're less mature. The more they
advance into their late twenties, the more disenchanted
these young women seem to become about the pool
of prospective mates and the likelihood of finding a
husband.[18]

Danielle Crittenden, author of the book *What Our Mothers Didn't Tell Us* notes that "when a woman is young and reasonably attractive, men will pass through her life with the regularity of subway trains; even when the platform is empty, she'll expect another to be coming along soon. . . . But if a woman remains single until her age creeps up past thirty, she may find herself tapping at her watch and staring down the now mysteriously empty tunnel, wondering if there hasn't been a derailment or accident somewhere along the line."[19]

The Hidden Details No One's Talking About

I was recently discussing this topic with two of my young coworkers. One is single and in her late twenties (and not currently dating anyone), and the other is in her early thirties and recently married. Both confirmed that the delayed marriage trend is, in fact, a reality and creating a devastating amount of heartache among our Christian single women. They recounted their own panic over the realization that the prospects for women decrease as the years increase. They shared about the common frustration they and their friends experienced with Christian single men their own age and their propensity to date younger women. They said that for many of their friends, the decision no longer centered around whether to sign up on eHarmony and other dating sites—many had long given in and reluctantly signed up—the decision was whether to broaden their prospect pool by marking that they were willing to be "matched" with older, divorced, or widowed men. They were coming to terms with the sobering reality that the single men their age seemed to be more preoccupied with younger women. The younger women, in turn, adored the attention from men who were more settled and stable in their careers than their male counterparts in their mid-twenties. I'm sure none of them ever imagined when they were younger that it would come to this. Crittenden says:

> This is when the cruelty of her singleness really sets in, when she becomes aware of the fine print in the unwritten bargain she has cut with the opposite sex. Men will outlast her. Men, particularly successful men, will be attractive and virile into their fifties. They can start families whenever they feel like it. So long as a woman was willing to play a man's game at dating—playing the field, holding men to no expectations of permanent commitment—men would be around; they would even live with her! But the moment she began exuding that desire for something more permanent, they'd vanish.[20]

A Mother's Response: Telling Our Daughters the Truth

What is a Christian parent to tell her daughter? Certainly, we don't tell her to settle for the first young man who looks her way. But shouldn't we at least tell her to be open and mindful of marriage at a much younger age? Further, shouldn't we level with her about the culture's message that "you can have it all—your timetable and your terms" and inform her that it's nothing more than a lie? Marriage and motherhood are not something that you scribble on a "to-do" list next to "get milk" and "pick up dry cleaning."

> **M**arriage and motherhood are not something that you scribble on a "to-do" list next to "get milk" and "pick up dry cleaning."

When you consider that the average age of marriage was around twenty years for women in 1950, combined with the fact that parents were more strict regarding their daughters entering dating relationships in their teen years, it wasn't unreasonable to expect a young lady (or young man) to put their hormones on hold for a handful of years. Today we essentially expect them to put their hormones aside for a decade or more while they build their careers, enjoy their singlehood, and become more independent. And I wonder exactly how many of us would have been able to meet that challenge?

It seems to me that if God felt it best to delay marriage into the latter part of your twenties, He would also see fit to delay the hormonal urge to want to have sex. Or perhaps it was never His intent to delay marriage in an effort to "become more independent," "enjoy singlehood," and "build our careers." Author Danielle Crittenden points out how years of independence from the single years can actually backfire. "By spending years and years living entirely for yourself, thinking only about yourself, and having responsibility to no one but yourself, you end up inadvertently extending the introverted existence of a teenager deep into middle age."[21] She also notes that "the traits that are forgivable in a twenty-year-old—the constant wondering about who you are and what you will be; the readiness to chuck one thing, or person, for another and move on—are less attractive in a thirty-two-year-old. More often what results is a middle-aged person who retains all the irritating self-absorption of an adolescent without gaining any of the redeeming qualities of maturity."[22]

Crittenden assessed the current dilemma facing our daughters by suggesting that women are leading their lives backwards. She says, "We squander our youth and our sexual passion upon men who are not worth it, and only when we are older and less sexually powerful do we try and find a man who is worth it. We start our careers in our twenties, when we are at our most physically fertile and yet are neither old enough nor experienced enough to get anywhere professionally. Then we try to have babies when our jobs are finally starting to go somewhere but our bodies are less receptive to pregnancy."[23]

Further, she concludes this summary with timely advice that we, as Christian parents would be wise to pass along to our daughters:

> Let's say she started thinking about it at the time she
> went to college. She could date a number of men in her
> late teens and early twenties, and feel less pressure to
> sleep with them if she knew she would soon be choosing
> one of them. And by taking marriage more seriously, at
> an earlier age, she would be less likely to waste her time,
> or her heart, upon men with whom she couldn't imagine
> spending the rest of her life. [AMEN!] If other young
> women followed her example, the shrinkage in the number
> of sexually available young women would have its effect on
> men: Sexual conquests would be harder, depriving them
> of their current easy ability to persuade women to share
> their beds without sharing their lives. [AMEN again!] By
> marrying earlier rather than later, a woman could also have
> children when she's most physically ready for them, and
> without much disruption to her career, if she plans to have
> one.[24]

Looking for Love Versus Waiting for Love

I find it difficult to bite my tongue when visiting with darling Christian women in their late twenties and thirties who lament their single status and then go on to tell me they attend a church with little or no singles department, hang out with the girls on the weekend, and make little to no effort to mix in Christian coed settings. Then they shrug it off with a casual, "Oh well, I guess God will bring him to my doorstep when the time is right." Sometimes they even compare their sit-back-and-wait philosophy to biblical accounts like Genesis 29 where God does a little divine match-making when He brings Jacob and Rachel together at a well while watering their sheep. No doubt, God is in the business of special deliveries, but doesn't it seem a tad presumptuous to *expect* Him to deliver? Let us not also forget another account in the book of Ruth where Naomi does a little matchmaking of her own between her widowed daughter-in-law and Boaz. In Ruth 3:3–4 she says, "Wash and perfume yourself, and put on your best clothes. Then go down to the threshing floor, but don't let him know you are there until he has finished eating and drinking. When he lies down, note the place where he is lying. Then go and uncover his feet and lie down." Her willingness to follow her mother-in-law's wisdom earns her a marriage proposal.

There is a balance between going on an all-out husband hunt and just sitting back and waiting for a knock on the door. Dawn Eden, author of *The Thrill of the Chaste*, offers this word of wisdom to single women: "Well, the first thing to do, obviously, if you want to meet your future husband, is to get out of the house."[25] If you want a new car, go where the new cars are. If you want to meet single Christian men, go where the single Christian men are. If God is leading you to stay at your church with no singles department, you're going to have to find other ways to meet singles.

> Our daughters need to know that God's timing works best when we abide by His timetable rather than our own.

I am certainly not suggesting that we manipulate God's timing or will regarding marriage. For some girls, it will not be in God's will for them to marry. For yet others God may choose to delay marriage. Our daughters need to know that God's timing works best when we abide by His timetable rather than our own. Romans 12:2 reminds us, "Don't copy the behavior and customs of this world, but let God transform you into a new person by changing the way you think. Then you will learn to know God's will for you which is good and pleasing and perfect" (NLT). Whether marriage is part of God's will for your daughter or not, she needs to know that the most important relationship she will ever have is her relationship with Jesus Christ. When she makes her relationship with Christ the focus, everything else will fall into place. Marriage may or may not be a part of her future, but if her eyes are on Jesus and her heart beats first and foremost for Him, the outcome won't matter.

CHAPTER FIFTEEN

Hooking Up, Shacking Up, and Other Marriage Busters

Recently I was catching up with a college girl who is a friend of the family, and I asked her what the biggest adjustment was for her when she went away to college. Without hesitation, she replied, "I can't believe how many girls hook up. And it's not just the wild girls like it was in high school. A lot of the church girls hook up, too. It's like no one dates anymore, and the girls don't even expect the guys to ask them out." I have written about the hook-up trend before, and it saddens me that so few girls will experience the thrill of being asked out on a date, courted, and pursued. The few girls who acknowledge they are worth it and make dating a requirement in the "get to know you" process are often harassed (or simply ignored) by the guys. Many guys rationalize, "Why go to all that trouble and spend my money on a girl when there are so many others to choose from who won't require it?" Even in dating, sex isn't put off for long. A survey conducted by the National Marriage Project to gauge the attitudes of young singles regarding "mating and dating" revealed that sex on the third date (or after a couple of weeks of meeting) is typical for a more serious relationship. "If you wait too long," says one guy, "they think you're not interested."[1]

Of course, one would hope the Christian boys are different, but the truth is, they're fighting the same raging hormones as the next guy. It's awfully difficult to resist something that promises instant pleasure and is free for the taking. I'm not justifying it but rather stating the facts as I see them. Countless Christian girls who have committed themselves to purity have shared that there seems to be a real shortage of Christian guys who appreciate that commitment . . . well, at least until it's time to settle down for marriage.

I have tried to drill home the mantra to my daughter, "If you're not worth dating, he's not worth kissing." Of course, this doesn't mean she owes a guy a kiss if he takes her on a date and spends a little money on her. My point is, there are too many Christian girls who have accepted that hooking up for a sample make-out session is a necessary litmus test to determine future compatibility. Compatibility should be explored in a friendship relationship. Once a physical spark has been ignited, it's hard to tame the fire and "get to know" the person apart from the kiss and the hopes of what might follow that kiss. Unfortunately, we have a long way to go in shifting the attitudes of young people when it comes to dating versus mating. In fact, the study I cited above found that the men and women in the focus groups rarely volunteered the word *love* or used the phrase "falling in love." Instead of "love," they spoke about "sex" and "relationships." Clearly, there is a disconnect when it comes to dating and the concept of falling in love.[2]

As long as our culture continues to peddle the pro hook-up message and, further, leads our girls to believe it is an expression of "girl power," plenty of girls will be ready and willing to oblige the boys with casual sex. When it comes to dating, the boys will be off the hook, unless we encourage our daughters to set the bar high and expect to be respected. Clearly this is a conversation we need to have not only with our daughters but with our sons as well.

Shacking Up: Premarriage Courtship?

Since 1960, the number of unmarried couples who live together has increased more than tenfold.[3] What was considered immoral and unacceptable fifty years ago has now shifted to become somewhat of an expectation, especially among men. The study by the National Marriage Project found that most of the participants view cohabitation in a favorable light, and almost all the men agreed with the view that you should not marry a woman until you have lived with her first.[4] Nearly 70 percent of those who get married lived together first.[5]

Since 1960, the number of unmarried couples who live together has increased more than tenfold.

What is the appeal or the reasoning behind the decision to shack up? The study above sheds light on the three most common reasons cited by unmarried singles:

1. They hope to find out more about the habits, character, and fidelity of a partner.
2. They want to test compatibility, possibly for future marriage.
3. They want to live together as a way of avoiding the risks of divorce or being "trapped in an unhappy marriage."[6]

There seems to be much confusion and miscommunication regarding any "perceived" benefits of cohabitation. Ironically, cohabitation actually increases the risk that the relationship will break up before marriage. A National Marriage Project report states that "many studies have found that *those who live together before marriage have less satisfying marriages* and a considerably higher chance of eventually breaking up." One reason is that people who cohabit may be more skittish of commitment and more likely to call it quits when problems arise. In addition, the act of living together may lead to attitudes that make happy marriages more difficult. The findings of one recent study, for example, suggest "there may be less motivation for cohabiting partners to develop their conflict resolution and support skills."[7] Those who do go on to marry have higher separation and divorce rates.[8] And whether they go on to marry their cohabitation partner or someone else, they are more likely to have extramarital affairs. When it comes to staying faithful, married partners have higher rates of loyalty every time. One study done over a five-year period, reported in *Sexual Attitudes and Lifestyles*, indicates that 90 percent of married women were monogamous, compared to 60 percent of cohabiting women.

Statistics were even more dramatic with male faithfulness: 90 percent of married men remained true to their brides while only 43 percent of cohabiting men stayed true to their partners.[9] Another study, published in the *Journal of Marriage and the Family* that analyzed the relationships of 1,235 women ages twenty to thirty-seven, found that women who cohabited before marriage were 3.3 times more likely to have a secondary sex partner after marriage.[10] Not to mention they have more frequent disagreements, fights, and exposure to violence.[11] Depression rates are more than three times higher for those who cohabit than for those who marry.[12] Additionally, those who choose cohabitation under the assumption that the sex will be better than "married" sex should take note: according to a large-scale national study, married couples have both more and better sex than do their unmarried counterparts. Not only do they have sex more often, but they enjoy it more, both physically and emotionally.[13]

The verdict is in: living together before marriage is damaging to your physical, spiritual, and emotional health and can impact the health of your future marriage whether you end up marrying the person you lived with or someone else. Yet our young people continue to buy the culture's lies, never questioning the error of their ways and the fallout it may produce in the years to come. And allowing men the ready option to "try marriage out" by living together first further delays marriage during the prime childbearing years for our young women. The familiar saying, "Why buy the cow if you can get the milk for free," certainly applies here. I continue to be amazed that we hear little, if any, outcry over the devastating impact the sexual revolution has had on women. With little to no external pressures to wed for men, women are the real losers in this deal. Is this really liberation? Ironically, the girls with true "girl power" are the ones who say no to sex outside of marriage and raise the bar high for their potential suitors. Seems mighty powerful to me when a young lady draws a line in the sand and refuses to give away her heart emotionally and give away her body physically outside of God's perfect timing. Does your daughter know about this brand of girl power?

> With little to no external pressures to wed for men, women are the real losers in this deal.

Let me also confess something that I have kept to myself for some time and have dared not say (until now) for fear it might possibly hurt the feelings of those who lived together outside of marriage. I share it because I feel it could benefit our daughters in an effort to dissuade them from cohabiting prior to marriage, especially given that a majority of men have come to expect it. I recently shared with my daughter that I cannot imagine that the joy of planning a wedding, honeymoon, and setting up a household would be the same for those who have already lived together, slept together, and set up a household prior to marriage. What's the thrill of taking a honeymoon when so many of these couples have already taken vacations together and shared a bed? Why bother with the showers when they already have a toaster, microwave, and dishes? Why pay for an expensive ceremony to say "I do" in front of their friends and family when they've been pretending at marriage for some time. I'm sorry if this sounds harsh, but should any of my three children opt to live together outside of marriage and then decide to marry for real, this momma won't be paying a dime toward wedding expenses or a honeymoon. I will take that child aside well in advance and quietly yet strongly suggest that their choice to shack up in a pseudo, pretend marriage should disqualify them from partaking in the traditional wedding benefits. Dad and I will be there for the ceremony should we believe this is, in fact, God's intended spouse for our child, but we won't open our wallets.

An exception perhaps would be a sincere confession of wrongdoing followed by repentance where they move out and commit to secondary virginity for a suitable period of time. To me, living together outside of marriage falls into the same category as pregnancy outside of marriage. A small, private ceremony is in order, but a traditional wedding with all the bells and whistles would seem inappropriate and distasteful. I hope the occasion doesn't arise where this sort of tough love is necessary, but I'm willing to take the stand should we be faced with the situation.

I am living proof that those who commit to secondary virginity can still experience the joy and anticipation that was intended for their wedding day. Opening the shower gifts and dreaming about setting up our household together, planning the honeymoon and looking forward to the moment when we could finally lie next to one another in the same bed, the excitement of returning to our apartment after the honeymoon and being carried over the threshold—these were unforgettable memories. Truly this was God's intent all along—you play house only after you swap your vows and not a moment before. And that is the hope I would offer any young lady who has strayed from God's path and forfeited His perfect timing. It's never too late to begin again. Never.

Divorce: Not So Happily Ever After

Nearly half of all marriages will end up in divorce. Surprisingly, the divorce statistics remain about the same for Christians as they do for non-Christians. While most parents are somewhat familiar with that statistic, few actually talk over the consequences of divorce with their children. Of course, when you consider that nearly half of the parents are (or have been) divorced, you can understand why broaching the topic could be awkward and uncomfortable, to say the least. However, if we truly want our children to experience God's best in marriage, we must educate them to the damaging consequences of divorce.

I think most would agree that divorce is far too common in our culture today; and, due to its ready availability, many rush into the decision. As most of us know, every marriage will experience ups and downs. Research (using a large national sample of people) found that 86 percent of people who were unhappily married in the late 1980s yet opted to stay in the marriage, indicated when interviewed five years later that they were happier. Further, three-fifths of the formerly unhappily married couples rated their marriages as either "very happy" or "quite happy."[14] It certainly makes you wonder how many marriages could be salvaged if couples were not so quick to rush into divorce.

Far too often we hear that a couple has decided to divorce because they "are no longer in love," "are incompatible," or "have irreconcilable differences." For Christians, Scripture clearly states that the only support for divorce is infidelity or when an unbelieving partner walks away. Even then, divorce does not have to be the option, and in many cases the marriage can be saved with the help of counseling. We all know of couples where one partner is willing to do whatever it takes to make the marriage work, but for whatever reasons the other partner is not. I have several friends who fall into this category, and my heart breaks for the pain they have experienced. They would be among the first to share that divorce produces devastating consequences for all involved.

If you are reading this and have experienced divorce, I encourage you to put aside the reasons behind your own divorce for the sake of having a candid and honest discussion with your daughter about the consequences of divorce. I doubt that any divorced mother would want her daughter to also become a divorce statistic. We must be willing to roll up our sleeves and fight if we wish to break the chains of divorce. The truth is, certain key factors decrease the likelihood of divorce. As mothers, we owe it to our daughters (and our sons) to make sure they are aware of the following factors.

Ten Proven Factors That Will Increase the Likelihood of a Happy and Healthy Marriage and Decrease the Likelihood of Divorce

1. Save sex for marriage.
2. Have a solid relationship with Christ, and marry someone with the same foundation of faith.
3. Do not consider divorce as an option and refuse to make it a part of your vocabulary.

4. Get a college education.

5. Do not marry as a teen.

6. Understand that every marriage will come with difficulties. Seek to serve more than be served.

7. Marry someone with similar values, background, and life goals.

8. Do not live together prior to marriage.

9. Have children after you are married. (**Note:** Should pregnancy occur outside of marriage, the right thing to do is have the child. Abortion should not be an option.)

10. Refuse to settle for anyone less than God's best: a guy who has proven to be a strong spiritual leader capable of leading and providing for a family.

In addition to the above factors, it has also been found that marrying someone whose family of origin is intact also increases the likelihood of a happy and healthy marriage.[15]

Does this mean that we tell our daughters that under no circumstances should they marry someone from a divorced home? No! Children cannot be blamed for their parents' mistakes. I know plenty of adults who, because of their parents' painful divorce and the damage it caused along the way, are all the more determined to make their own marriages work. The key is recognizing that it may be more difficult for our daughters if they come from a divorced home or marry someone from a divorced home. The overall goal is making sure they are aware that those coming from divorced homes have usually not been exposed to a healthy marriage environment and will not have a baseline of comparison when it comes to their own marriage.

If Your Daughter Is from a Divorced Home

Judith Wallerstein, a well-known authority who has written on the impact of divorce on children, studied 131 people who, as children, experienced the divorce of their parents. In her landmark report, *The Unexpected Legacy of Divorce*, she says: "Divorce is a life-transforming experience. After divorce, childhood is different. Adolescence is different. Adulthood—with the decision to marry or not and have children or not—is different. Whether the final outcome is good or bad, the whole trajectory of an individual's life is profoundly altered by the divorce experience."[16] I am not sharing this information to beat you over the heads if you are divorced, and as I mentioned before, I have friends who have experienced divorce and honestly did not want it or see it coming. My heart aches for anyone who has experienced divorce, and especially for the children. We must address the impact of divorce on children so you will be better equipped in having the necessary conversation with your daughter regarding the truth about divorce. We must do everything in our power to spare our daughters from the painful consequences of divorce.

If your daughter's biological father is not living in the home, the situation can impact her future relationships with the opposite sex. Ginny Olson, author of the book *Teenage Girls: Exploring Issues Adolescent Girls Face and Strategies to Help Them*, noted that for such girls, "Her primary role model for male-female relationships is missing and it can be difficult for her to figure out how to build healthy relationships with men."[17] She cited a landmark research study that looked at how girls who were raised in a variety of family contexts related to their fathers, especially situations where the father was absent. The study examined girls who were raised by married mothers, widowed mothers, and divorced mothers. She found that, in comparison to girls raised by both parents in the home, "girls whose mothers were widowed were more guarded and reserved in their dealings with men. They set high standards for potential mates. And the girls who were raised by divorced mothers flirted more and began dating at a much earlier age than the girls from the other two groups."[18] She suggested that fathers "need to be encouraged to pursue communication with their daughters. The more relational a dad is, asking questions and keeping the lines of communication open, the less likely it is that his daughter will become involved in risky behavior in her later teen years."[19] If this is not a possibility in your daughter's life, consider exposing her to another male family member who is a positive example of a godly husband and father. It would also help to address the matter with her *before* she becomes a teen and have an honest and frank conversation with her about her increased susceptibility to seek out male attention at an early age. Maybe you were the girl I am describing and experienced the same thing. Tell her. Be honest with her and, most importantly, open up the lines of communication so she will be comfortable discussing it with you in the years to come. Don't wait for her to come to you; she likely never will.

Take the initiative to discuss the matter and continue to talk about it even as she gets older. Stay engaged and don't lighten up when it comes to drawing boundaries in dating. In addition, make a concentrated effort to speak highly of the institution of marriage and consider pointing out positive examples of godly Christian marriages in your church. If possible, expose her to those marriages so she will have an idea of what a good marriage looks like and see it as a blessing rather than a burden. In being honest with her, you will not come across as a failure. As mothers we must take advantage of teachable moments even if it means that, sometimes, we are unfortunately part of the teachable moment—just as I have been when it comes to discussing with my own children the consequences of sex outside of marriage.

A New PR Campaign for Marriage: The Good News No One's Talking About

Most teens say they expect to marry (77 percent of boys; 84.5 percent of girls), and they further list "having a good marriage and family life" as "extremely important" (70 percent of boys; 82 percent of girls).[20] Unfortunately, our young people, and especially our girls, will hear little about the benefits of marriage. When was the last time you heard the media address the overwhelming and consistent findings by such reputable sources as the *Journal of Marriage and the Family* and the *American Journal of Sociology* that "married persons, both men and women, are on average considerably better off than all categories of unmarried persons (never married, divorced, separated, and widowed) in terms of happiness, satisfaction, physical health, longevity, and most aspects of emotional health"?[21] Given that God created marriage, should it really come as a surprise that marriage is, in fact, good for you?

Mothers, it's up to us to extol the benefits of marriage to our daughters as a God-ordained union that can bring much happiness and, most importantly, honor to Him. The National Marriage Project states that the burden of changing attitudes about marriage rests with *parents*. "Contrary to the popular notion that the media is chiefly responsible for young people's attitudes about mating and marriage, available evidence strongly suggests that young people get many of their ideas and models of marriage from parents and the parental generation."[22] That's the good news. The bad news is that the same study also found that "many parents have had almost nothing good to say about marriage and often say nothing at all,"

> **M**ake a concentrated effort to speak highly of the institution of marriage and consider pointing out positive examples of godly Christian marriages in your church.

claiming the negativism and/or silence could be due to "the parental generation's own marital problems and failures."[23]

Further, when polling young people about their attitudes regarding marriage, many in the study have unfortunately grown up with unhappily married or divorced parents. They have no baseline for determining what a healthy marriage even looks like and have therefore been left with a tainted picture. Some even described a good marriage as "the opposite of my parents."[24] Ouch. Moreover, a number of participants in the study said they received "no advice" or "mainly negative advice" about marriage from their "parents and relatives."[25] Reading that last statement should cause a collective shudder among us all. How can we break the chains of this dysfunctional cycle when many are, in fact, perpetuating and encouraging it?

No doubt, many reading this have experienced their fair share of hurt and pain in marriage. No one ever said marriage was easy, but can we put aside any hurt and pain we may have experienced and focus, rather, on God's intent for marriage? I know this is a tricky balance and will require some moms to be blatantly honest with their daughters and say, "You know honey, I realize that Dad and I haven't modeled (didn't model) the best marriage to you, but the truth is, God intended marriage to be a wonderful thing." It may mean putting pride aside and even pointing out healthy marriages that could perhaps serve as tangible examples to our daughters. It might even be necessary to confess mistakes you may have made in an effort to dissuade her from making the same mistakes. The problem is too many with broken marriages are claiming marriage, in general, is the mistake. We must distinguish that God doesn't create mistakes, but people, in fact, make mistakes. Most failed marriages can be traced back to mistakes made by both parties and a failure to adhere to God's standards of marriage. When His standards are not followed, marriages will suffer and often times even fail. If this is your case, can you claim responsibility for your mistakes and still speak highly about the institution of marriage? Of course, if you are a Christian who is married to an unbeliever, you can point out to your daughter God's counsel for Christians not to be "unequally yoked" with unbelievers but do so in a manner that would not dishonor your husband. God can heal any marriage, and prayer is an essential part of that process.

I realize some women may be reading this who followed God's standards and, for whatever reason, your once godly husband chose to walk away or chase after a life of sin. I personally know several women who experienced this painful misfortune, and my heart breaks for them. Even though they have had a sour experience, they have not allowed the experience to sour their attitudes regarding marriage. They have worked hard to speak highly of marriage and make sure that their children are not left with a negative impression. This is an especially tricky balance when it comes to pointing out mistakes made by the other party, and I caution you to refrain from sharing too many details or divulging information that could put a strain on the relationship they have with their father.

And for those of us who currently have healthy marriages, have we done our part in talking it up in the hearing of our daughters? Does your daughter know how much you value marriage? Does she see you exhibit affection and swap caring words? Does she witness positive examples of conflict/resolution and confession/forgiveness? Trust me, I am personally convicted by the weight of those words. I love being married. Sure, it's tough at times, and my husband and I have had our fair share of challenges, but I wouldn't trade it for anything. And on that note, I think I'll go sit my daughter down and make sure she knows that. Marriage is a blessing from the Lord. Moms, if we want to see a new PR campaign for marriage take place, it will start in our own homes . . . beginning with each of us.

CHAPTER SIXTEEN

When I Grow Up,
I Want to Be a Mom

I f you had asked me when I was a little girl what I wanted to be when I grew up, I would have likely answered, "A mom." I loved pretending that my dolls were real and tucking them into their plastic cradles at night. I loved changing their outfits throughout the day and feeding them their bottle with the fake milk that would disappear when you tipped it to their mouths. I loved pushing the toy stroller down the sidewalk and pretending I was just like the real mommies out taking their babies for a walk.

The motherhood dream continued into grade school, and I recall conversations with friends where we would talk about how many children we wanted, what sex they would be, and what we would name them. I wanted twin girls, and I was going to name them "Tiffany" and "Stephanie." So much for that! My friends and I looked forward to the day when we would be old enough to babysit and take care of real babies.

Something happened between those years and high school. During the seventies and eighties the women's liberation movement was in full swing, and girls were ODed with the culture's message that building a career was the key to true fulfillment. By college I considered myself a feminist, and motherhood quickly became an afterthought—something I might think about after the career is in full swing if it allows any spare time for a husband and children. Even the girls who still held onto the marriage and motherhood dream dared not admit it. You may as well stamp "uneducated doormat" across their foreheads. Women had come too far to revert back to the days of caring for cooing babies. We had college degrees and were more bent on carrying a briefcase than a diaper bag. Besides, why bother with all that college and invest so much financially if we weren't planning to use it? That was the pervasive thought of the day during my college years.

> We had college degrees and were more bent on carrying a briefcase than a diaper bag.

When I became a Christian in my junior year of college, I began to realize how I had bought into the lies of the culture. Slowly but surely God began to ignite my heart once again to the childhood dream of marriage and motherhood. It was OK to dream again. Not that I put my career aspirations aside, but rather I traded in my own blueprint for the future and handed the reins of control over to the Lord. And it's a good thing I did. Four months after I was married at the age of twenty-three, to the shock of both my husband and myself, I discovered I was pregnant. I was going to be a *mother*.

I imagine that you also have similar sentiments about mother-hood, or you likely would not have picked up a book on necessary conversations you must have with your daughter. And I'm sure it goes without saying that you hope your daughter someday experi-ences the joys of marriage and motherhood, should this be part of God's plan. On that note, let's take a look at some ways we can pass along the dream of motherhood to our daughters.

Delayed Childbearing

I realize I touched on this to some degree in chapter 15 when I discussed delayed marriage, but allow me to go into more detail in this chapter regarding its domino effect on delayed childbearing. According to a 2004 report relying on US Census data, a growing percentage of women today are childless. In 1976, one out of ten women in their early forties was childless as compared to one out of five in 2004.[1] Perhaps one of the most interesting (and frightening) books I read in my research for this chapter was a book I have cited in a previous chapter, *Unprotected: A Campus Psychiatrist Reveals How Political Correctness in Her Profession Endangers Every Student*, by an author under the pen, "Anonymous, M.D." This author chose the cloak of anonymity for fear of losing her job over sharing her firsthand witness of the damaging toll the sexual revolution is hav-ing on our young women. This brave doctor reveals the extent to which she and others in her profession are trained to counsel young women to take preventive measures to ward off such distant ail-ments as osteoporosis but are not allowed to comment on behaviors or variables that could, in fact, impact future fertility. In chapter 9 I discussed at length several STDs that can lead to infertility and are oftentimes undetected until later on down the road after the damage has been done.

Now stop for a minute and think about the popular ads for milk that are almost guaranteed to appear in every fashion magazine on the market. Most of us can even finish the line, "Milk. It does a body ____" (good). What celebrity hasn't posed with the familiar milk mustache in one of the ads for this campaign? The message of the campaign is clear: Drink milk; it's good for you. Where in the magazines or on TV are the positive PR ads that encourage girls to avoid casual sex hookups in an effort to protect future fertility?

Or what about the ads that warn young women about some of the side effects stemming from delayed marriage and childbirth? I'm not saying we should discourage young ladies from pursuing careers, but I think we owe it to them to inform them of what the medical community has been aware of for some time. In spite of the culture's negative attitudes regarding marriage and motherhood, most women expect and hope that they will someday marry and have children. However, a 2001 survey showed 89 percent of young, high-achieving women also believed they would be able to get pregnant into their forties.[2] Another study found that women have an excellent understanding of birth control, but they "overestimate the age at which fertility declines."[3]

The Truth Regarding Delayed Marriage and Motherhood

- If you are a healthy thirty-year-old woman, you have about a 20 percent chance per month to get pregnant. By age forty, however, your chance is only about 5 percent per month.[4]
- At age thirty-nine the chance of a live birth after an IVF attempt is 8 percent. By age forty-four, it falls to 3 percent.[5]
- The actual rate for successful birth using frozen eggs is closer to 2.5 percent.[6]

- If a woman conceives at age thirty-eight, the possibility of miscarriage has tripled, the rate of stillbirth has doubled, and the risk of genetic abnormality is six times as great.[7] Additionally, the pregnancy is more likely to be complicated by high blood pressure or diabetes, and the baby is more likely to be premature or low birth weight.[8]

> At age thirty-nine the chance of a live birth after an IVF attempt is 8 percent.

- Women treated for infertility suffer from anxiety and depression as severely as patients who have been diagnosed with cancer or cardiac disease.[9]

We've all heard the warnings about aging and a woman's eggs getting old, but some women are taking their fears to the next level by putting their eggs on ice, just to play it safe. Oocyte cryopreservation, or egg freezing, used to be available only to young women facing chemotherapy or suffering from illnesses that might make them infertile, but it has found a new market in the burgeoning population of single women. Extend Fertility, a growing company started by Harvard MBA Christy Jones, offers egg freezing to any woman with healthy ovaries and about fifteen grand to spend on a mere chance at extending fertility.[10]

What sort of woman would opt for such a procedure? Consider Tessa who, in an interview with the *Daily Mail*, stated, "I can devote time to my career, take my time finding Mr. Right and know that when I deem the time is right, even if I am menopausal, I can still have my own baby."[11] She further claims that she was "brought up to believe that having a career, being independent and earning my own living were the most important things in life."[12] Interesting how marriage and motherhood didn't make her first cut on the "important life accomplishments" list. I sure hope she doesn't live to regret her priorities.

Perhaps she should heed the warning of Dr. Zev Rosenwaks, director of The Center for Reproductive Medicine and Infertility, the world-renowned infertility clinic at New York Weill Cornell. In a *New York Times* editorial piece addressing the problem of infertility due to delayed marriage and motherhood, he had this to say:

> The non-stop media parade of midlife women producing offspring is stunning. . . . These stories are about the fortunate ones: they beat the odds. . . . As an infertility specialist, I often see women . . . who have been lulled into a mistaken belief that there is a medical technology that will allow women to have their genetic children whenever they choose. . . . In our eagerness to outwit time, the media have made a bestseller out of the freshly minted fiction of "rewinding the biological clock." We can't and we haven't.[13]

The former director of RESOLVE, a support network for couples coping with infertility, reports: "I can't tell you how many people we've had on our help line, crying and saying they had no idea how much fertility drops as you age."[14] Yet many of these same women are likely knowledgeable about the preventive measures you can take to avoid contracting osteoporosis or skin cancer! Not that there hasn't been an attempt to get the word out to young women regarding factors that can lead to infertility. The American Society of Reproductive Medicine (ASRM) sponsored a campaign in 2001 called Protect Your Fertility. The ads highlighted the four major causes of infertility: advancing age, sexually transmitted diseases, smoking, and unhealthy weight.[15] However, you probably don't remember seeing the ads because the campaign ended up being run aground by the National Organization for Women (NOW) before it could ever get feet. NOW argued that the campaign sent a negative message to women who might want to delay or skip childbearing. Hmmm. . . . And what about the women who *don't* want to delay or skip childbearing? Mall and theater managers refused to make space available for the ads, and thus the campaign died.[16]

No wonder the waiting rooms of fertility clinics are bursting at the seams with women in their thirties and forties who were led to believe they had nothing to worry about. We don't see the heartache behind those visits, the tears shed over a failed procedure, or the endless shots and pills that are required, not to mention the money spent for a shot-in-the-dark chance at motherhood. No, instead, we continue to see the lucky ones who have the money at their disposal to increase their luck even further. No wonder so many women are bitter when they discover the truth . . . the hard way.

In addition to other factors I have discussed prior to this chapter that can lead to delayed marriage (hooking up, cohabitation, sexual promiscuity leading to STDs), we must also add this one to the docket—the purposeful postponement of marriage and mother-hood for the sake of career-building. Albert Mohler, president of Southern Baptist Theological Seminary and host of a nationwide radio show "devoted to engaging contemporary culture with the biblical truth," had this to say in a blog on the topic:

> A woman's peak years of fertility and childbearing run from
> the late teens to her early 30s. . . . In the United States,
> the average age of first marriage for a woman is over 26—
> already well into her years of peak fertility. Add to that the
> impact of the contraceptive revolution and the fact that
> most of these women delay childbearing even further. . . .
> To a considerable extent, the fertility crisis for women is a
> crisis of delayed marriage and delayed motherhood. Women

have been sold a lie—that they can have it all. The hard reality is that none of us, male or female, can have it all.[17]

Children: Blessing or Burden?

Psalm 127 reminds us that children are a gift of the Lord and blessed is the man whose quiver is full of them. Yet ask any couple who dares to have a quiverful if the general public concurs that their brood is a "blessing." If you have four or more kids, chances are you have gotten your fair share of grimacing looks and perhaps even comments hinting that you're further contributing to the world's over-population problem. In the last fifty years the attitudes regarding children have radically shifted. Due to factors such as the delay of marriage, postponement of childbearing, and increased life expectancy, Americans now spend a smaller number of their expected lifetime years raising children and a larger number of years without children.[18]

As this shift has occurred, so have the attitudes regarding the season of life devoted to rearing children. Having and raising children was once considered a defining life purpose, whereas today it is often viewed as a disruption.[19] In addition to extending the years that make up the stage prior to having children and the years after raising the children, popular culture has glamorized the life of singles. (Think *Sex in the City* here.) These child-free years are often pitched as a sort of "last hurrah" before having to enter the stage of life where attention *must* be shared with someone else other than the almighty self. No doubt, children require seemingly

> Having and raising children was once considered a defining life purpose, whereas today it is often viewed as a disruption.

endless amounts of time and energy, but why does our culture view this as a disruption rather than a defining phase of life? Raising children has been the hardest challenge I have ever faced, but it has in turn, been one of the most rewarding phases of my life.

Further evidence that the public at large has begun to accept the culture's message that children are more of a burden than a blessing surfaced in a recent survey. According to the Pew Research Center, "having children" has fallen to eighth on a list of nine keys to happiness in marriage. Beating out the blessing of "having children" is "the sharing of household chores."[20] Wow. Popular radio host and counselor Dr. Laura Schlesinger notes on her blog that of the nine "qualities," only one anything to do with giving, and that is "having children." The remaining eight "keys to happiness in marriage" all have to do with getting. She sums up the severity of this finding with this statement: "When 50% more folks think that not taking one more bag of garbage to the curb than their spouse is more important to a marriage than combining love and energies into making a family, America is in trouble."[21]

While I seriously doubt that any of us view our children as a disruption, I think it is possible to unintentionally leave our children feeling like a burden. When my kids were small, God convicted my heart about whining and grumbling over parenting challenges in the hearing of my children. Whether it was over spilled milk or a baby who refused a morning nap in the early years, or a forgotten backpack or the never-ending shuttling to practices in the latter years, I began to realize that my children were mindful of my negative attitude. With the help of the Lord, I began to make a concentrated effort to focus on the blessing that my children are and, further, to express it in the hearing of my children. For example, just last week I told my fifteen-year-old son (and baby of the family) that I was going to miss shuttling him around when he started driving. Sure, a part of me will turn cartwheels when he has his own transportation, but honestly, I will miss the conversations we have had while riding in the car together.

I should also note that another extreme in parenting can be equally damaging—the parents who pour everything into their children and make them the focal point of their marriage. They base their own worth and value on their children's accomplishments and successes. In other words, the children become their one and only key to happiness in marriage. Of course, these are the parents who often find themselves lost and without direction when they become empty-nesters. They are faced with the task of reacquainting themselves with their spouse and developing other outside interests. As with most things, balance is the key.

> Children *are* a blessing from the Lord, and it's up to us to remind our daughters of that truth.

Children *are* a blessing from the Lord, and it's up to us to remind our daughters of that truth. When was the last time you told your children that they are a blessing? When was the last time they heard you say, "I love being a mom"? Children who know without a shadow of a doubt that they are blessings are more likely to view their own children as blessings. I would be willing to bet that our daughters' attitudes regarding motherhood will be most influenced by our own attitudes regarding motherhood. And our attitudes will be made known by both word and deed.

Career, Family, or Both?

Gloria Steinem was one of the key leaders of the feminist movement that originated in the 1960s. Steinem, along with others such as Betty Frieden, were pioneers in shifting attitudes among women when it came to women's liberation. Whether it was sexual liberation, liberation in the workforce, or liberation from the constraints of marriage and motherhood, they carried the banner high. While I commend the progress made for women when it comes to equal pay for equal work, the message of Steinem and her cohorts went far beyond that. Much of this liberation effort was to rail against the patriarchy and impart to women that their greatest joy comes from building a career and serving self—forgoing anything that may threaten to get in the way. Was this message successful? No doubt, it had an influence, but overall, women were not willing to give up marriage and motherhood as a whole (including Steinem, who herself eventually married in 2000 at the age of sixty-six). In a recent interview Steinem commented that female college students today are radically different from the feminist ideal she and others had envisioned.

She stated, "I've yet to be on a campus where most women weren't worrying about some aspect of combining marriage, children and a career."[22] As well they should be, I might add. The culture has done a bang-up job of carrying the "you can have it all!" banner to our young women but has failed to tell them *how* to have it all and live to tell about it. And apparently many young women are taking note that "having it all" is not all it's cracked up to be. Several years ago *The New York Times* reported that a growing number of college young women are aiming for full-time motherhood as a major career aspiration. And amazingly, the report focused on young women at some of the most elite universities in the country.[23]

> The culture has done a bang-up job of carrying the "you can have it all!" banner to our young women but has failed to tell them *how* to have it all and live to tell about it.

Albert Mohler commented on this trend in a blog post related to *The New York Times* article: "Much attention has been focused on career women who leave the work force to rear children. What seems to be changing is that while many women in college two or three decades ago expected to have full-time careers, their daughters, while still in college, say they have already decided to suspend or end their careers when they have children. . . . In effect, these young women are launching a counter-revolution to the trends of the last four decades."[24]

Now please know that the purpose of this chapter is not to extol the benefits of being a stay-at-home mother and make you feel guilty if you have a career. Having a career is not evil. In fact, the virtuous woman of Proverbs 31 had interests outside the home and was investing in real estate (v. 16), as well as making fine linen and selling it to the merchant ships (v. 24). I have absolutely no desire to partake in the "mommy wars" debate and line up on one side or the other. As someone who has been both a full-time stay-at-home mother and a working mother (part-time and full-time from home), I have been on both sides of the fence. My goal, rather, is to encourage mothers to be honest with their daughters and tell them the truth—*you can't really have it all.* Juggling a career and family is hard work. I have discovered firsthand: it's hard to *do it all* and *do it well.* I didn't say it was impossible, but we need to be honest here—it's *hard.* Let's put a stop to this ridiculous lie our culture has force-fed our daughters (and many of us, as well) in order that they might see it through a more realistic lens and be better equipped to make a fully informed choice.

For example, while working on this chapter, I struck up a conversation with a dear Christian mother whose daughter expressed a dream of someday becoming a physician. Her daughter also looks forward to the day she will marry and have children and wants to be engaged in her husband and children's lives. She had her daughter define *engaged* by asking her more pointed questions. Then this wise mother suggested that they ask female physicians if it is in fact possible to be a doctor and be engaged (as defined by her daughter) in your children's lives. I don't know what her daughter will ultimately decide to do, but I do know she is reevaluating her dream based on the answers she is gathering. Imagine if more mothers were helping their daughters do this sort of due diligence before they sink large sums of money and time into a career path that may leave them disillusioned in the end.

I have had many honest conversations with my daughter about her dreams for the future. She has told me with much certainty that her greatest dream is to be a wife and mother and that once the children come along she desires to stay home full-time. Regardless, I have encouraged her to have some sort of job skill under her belt to build security for a future that is uncertain and may not include marriage and motherhood. At the same time, knowing her desires on the front end aids us in better determining an area of interest in her academic pursuits that could possibly transition to a position that can be done at home or on a part-time basis if need be.

In addition, because she has expressed that it is important to her to stay at home with her children someday, I have also expressed the importance of making sure her future husband shares the same dream and willingly accepts the responsibility of becoming the sole provider in their home. Author Danielle Crittendon, in her book *What Our Mothers Didn't Tell Us*, shared an experience of a male attorney friend who married and after being reassured by his wife that she was "determined to make partner one day, like him" rather than be "stuck at home with a drooling infant," bought an expensive home with payments that assumed both their salaries. Only one problem. When they had their first baby, his wife changed her mind and decided not to return to her job. As many career-minded women have learned, "drooling infants" are often hard to part with when they are your own drooling infants. Her attorney friend expressed resentment over having to work longer than a sixty-hour workweek to make it work.[25]

That said, I also warned my daughter against making the common mistake many couples make in the first few years of marriage when they factor both incomes into the equation when buying a home or other items with long-term payment plans. Babies don't always come according to our own man-made timetables, and, couples are often caught off guard when parenthood arrives earlier than anticipated. This is especially true if they are locked into financial commitments that require two incomes. Learning to live on one income is not a bad idea even for those who are certain they want to continue working after having children. We all know women whose career dreams evaporated the first time they cradled their newborn baby in their arms and a new dream was birthed.

Most importantly, I have passed onto my daughter the biblical counsel that a mother should look "well to the ways of her household" (Prov. 31:27 ESV). Some women may be able to balance career and motherhood without sacrificing the quality of one or the other. Others, like myself, may work part-time from home in order to achieve the balance. (Even at that, I can assure you that the hours I currently devote to writing and ministry would not have been possible in my children's younger years.) Still others may desire to stay home full-time when they have children. Honestly, what works for one doesn't always work for another. I have met women who work full-time and are hopelessly devoted to their husbands and children and engaged in their lives. It's a challenge, but they somehow manage to pull it off. And on the flip side, I have met stay-at-home mothers who run

> We all know women whose career dreams evaporated the first time they cradled their newborn baby in their arms and a new dream was birthed.

themselves ragged volunteering for every cause in sight and end up with less time devoted to family at the end of the day than many career women. As mothers, our role is to guide our daughters to carefully think through their dreams for the future and help them examine whether or not they are realistic. Most importantly, we must emphasize the power of prayer and point them in the direction of One who knows them better than we or they know themselves. Only by praying and asking for God's wisdom (see James 1:5) and direction will our daughters find the balance they seek.

Girls Gone Wild Are a Dime a Dozen—Dare to Be Virtuous

CHAPTER SEVENTEEN

Bad Is the New Good

O h, how I long for the innocent days when Paris was just a city you hoped someday to visit and panties were a staple part of every girl's wardrobe. Or how about the days when that cute, freckle-faced girl in *Parent Trap* was known for being cute, freckle-faced, and a fabulous little actress rather than a cocaine-snorting, rehab grad. And the Olsen twins were back to living with their dad and Uncle Joey instead of nightclub hopping and dragging on a cigarette every time the camera flashes. And Vanessa Hudgens was not only the "good girl" in *High School Musical* but someone your daughter still thought was a "good girl" in real life. And Britney was just a Mouseketeer and singing in the church choir on the weekends. Remember those days? Back when it was good to be *good?*

Welcome to a new world where *bad* is the new *good*. Consider what Helen Grieco, director of California's National Organization for Women (NOW) said in defense of the spring break, boobie-flashing, *Girls Gone Wild* videos in an interview: "I think it's about being a rebel, and I don't think it's a bad notion. . . . Flashing your breasts on Daytona Beach says, 'I'm not a good girl. I think it's sexy to be a bad girl.'"[1] Yet another fine example of the "girl power" message that has been shoved down our daughters' collective throats. Since when is it considered "empowering" for college women to lift their bikini tops in response to the drunken catcalls of a bunch of immature frat boys? Did I miss something here?

> Welcome to a new world where *bad* is the new *good*.

Is it any wonder that our world is run amok with girls gone wild? Whether it's another news story about a beauty queen caught kissing another girl or an *American Idol* contestant with nude pictures on the Web, the glamorization of bad behavior is nonstop. As Hollywood plays rehab relay, it begs the question: Where are the good role models? Is the "good girl" persona now extinct, gone the way of shoulder pads and spiral perms? Possibly so, but it certainly doesn't mean we put our hands up and surrender.

Pantieless Pop Stars and the Never-Ending Rehab Relay

In a *Newsweek* poll, 77 percent of respondents say pop-star celebrities like Britney Spears, Paris Hilton, and Lindsay Lohan have too much influence on young girls.[2] However, perception and reality are two different things. In a related *Newsweek* article addressing the girls gone wild, Emma Boyce, a seventeen-year-old junior in high school, commented, "They've got great clothes and boyfriends. They seem to have a lot of fun." But the fascination stops short of admiration. Boyce went on to say, "My friends and I look at them and laugh at them. . . . Our lives seem pretty good by comparison. We're not going to rehab like Lindsay."[3] Mind you, her commentary was prior to Britney's self-implosion that followed shortly thereafter, including her head-shaving stunt and repetitive visits to a psych ward. Surely Miss Boyce has reevaluated her original assessment that these girls appear "to have a lot of fun."

I imagine if these pop stars were honest, they'd be the first to admit that "fun" is not a word to describe their plight. If you ever needed proof that money can't buy happiness, take a look at any one of the above pop stars and their respective infomercials for misery. The truth is, while the girls gone wild effect has touted bad as the new good, most level-headed girls are not rushing out to emulate the pop stars' brand of bad. There is nothing glamorous about rehab, drug and alcohol addictions, puking in hotel corridors, flashing your privates in public, shaving your head bald, losing custody of your two children, going to jail, having a sex tape leaked to the World Wide Web, and so on. Unfortunately, I fear the list will only get longer in the years to come. Should this pack of pop stars clean up their act (and I certainly pray they do), there are, no doubt, others waiting in the wings to rack up their own inventory of wild deeds.

Even though your daughter is not likely to be directly influenced by the misdeeds of these over-the-top, less-than-wholesome role models, it is possible that she will be left desensitized to what is considered godly and acceptable behavior for our young ladies. And that's where we come in. Our call is to point our daughters to a more virtuous standard of behavior as outlined by God in His Word.

Wanted: A Few Good Role Models

There was a day in the not-so-long-ago past that I would have sent Miley Cyrus a thank-you note for being a positive role model to young girls. It was during the time when other pop stars were self-imploding before our very eyes. Miley was a breath of fresh air, garnering fans worldwide with her wholesome character on the Disney hit, *Hannah Montana*. Had I written that thank-you note at the time, I would have thanked Miss Cyrus for having the decency to wear panties in public. I would have thanked her for knowing how to exit a limo gracefully without flashing the paparazzi her private parts. I would have thanked her for steering clear of the nightclubs and tattoo parlors. I would have thanked her for dressing with "decency and propriety" (1 Tim. 2:9). I would have thanked her for not having a cigarette in hand every time the camera flashes. I would have thanked her for having a track record that doesn't include rehab. I would have thanked her for being famous for an actual talent. I would have thanked her for singing songs with lyrics that don't make your grandma blush or your mom rush to change the channel on the radio. I would have thanked her for loving her parents. I would have thanked her for loving Jesus. And I would have thanked her for making my daughter smile at a time when most other pop stars left her shaking her head back and forth in utter disbelief.

That was then. Like you, I got my hopes up that perhaps there was one positive role model left in Hollywood, but it turns out that Miley Cyrus is human, after all. Like any one of us, she's a sinner saved by grace and capable of falling at any given moment. By the time this book hits the shelves, she could have gone the way of Britney, Lindsey, Paris, or one of the many other fallen pop stars. That is exactly why we should remind our daughters not to put anyone on a pedestal. Miss Cyrus has had some less than "picture-perfect" moments where her actions left some mommas angry and disappointed. Rather than wringing our hands and tearing our robes, let's take advantage of the teachable moments that can occur as a result of celebrity "role model" mishaps.

A Teachable Moment

Miley's mishaps began with some racy pictures that surfaced on the Web only to be followed by a Vanity Fair photo shoot where she bared her back for the camera. Many have chalked the pictures off to a momentary lapse in judgment while others have speculated that they signal a craving for rebellion and will only get worse over time. I pray that she will cling to her faith and turn it all around, but when it happened, I seized the opportunity to take advantage of a teachable moment with my own daughter. So, what is that teachable moment? Like Miley, my daughter owns a digital camera that came equipped with a memory card that holds more than five hundred pictures. Like most girls her age, she uploads the pictures straight to her Facebook page without a moment's thought. This was a driving force in why I tackled this very topic in my book, *Logged On and Tuned Out*, and encouraged parents to have some ground rules in place when it comes to uploading or sending pictures and videos via the Web or cell phone. (I even include a safety contract regarding picture and video uploading to go over with your child.)

My research on this topic led me to establish some rules with my own daughter such as, "Never upload pj or swimsuit shots or allow others to upload them on their pages." I also encourage my daughter (and sons) to take the time to pore over every picture and ask themselves, "Might this particular picture send a different message than I was intending to send to viewers?" Even so, my daughter has made some innocent mistakes along the way and had she had the notoriety of Miley Cyrus, some of her pictures might have raised an eyebrow or two. I recall one shot another girl took with my daughter in the background at a sleepover. She was wearing a camisole and leaning over, clueless at the time as to how the shot might look when loaded to her friend's online album. There have also been occasional pictures of her in swimwear taken by her friends that have surfaced on their albums. Of course, she asks them to remove the pictures, as per our rule. Oh, and if there were ever an incentive for parents to be engaged and knowledgeable about the pictures their children are uploading, consider the picture I recently saw in a teen girl's Facebook album who is a friend of my daughter's. The picture was of the young lady and her mother posing in their swimsuits on the beach while on vacation. I guarantee you that mother has no clue there is a swimsuit shot of her on the Web! Lord, have mercy! It left me with a renewed zeal never to remove my cover-up. It's waterproof, right?

True Role Models

Role models will come and go, so it's wise to keep a balanced perspective. Even those who appear to be good will disappoint at times (such as in the example above). While it's nice to be able to point our daughters to someone else's positive example, we want to make sure our daughters' admiration of the role model du jour doesn't go overboard and border on idol worship. And I would certainly caution mothers to exercise caution when it comes to looking to pop stars as role models. Most are not worthy of a following. Call attention to more realistic role models such as godly grandmothers or older young ladies or women in your church. In fact, in the late 1800s and early 1900s girls commonly spent their leisure time with godly women of all ages. Whether they were involved in a knitting circle or cooking alongside female family members, they were being informally mentored and exposed to a tangible picture of how the virtuous women of their day behaved.

Today much of the vision of mentoring our young ladies in the art of virtue has been lost. However, I am a big believer in the benefit of exposing our daughters to older godly female influences. My daughter has had the benefit of developing relationships with several young women in our congregation who are in their early twenties. A couple of them are married with younger children, which has afforded my daughter a glimpse of what may lie ahead. Additionally, during my daughter's senior year, she had the

Role models will come and go, so it's wise to keep a balanced perspective.

privilege of meeting monthly with a longtime mom friend of mine who is a staff wife at our church. I love that my daughter has the benefit of bouncing some things off someone else besides me.

As an additional twist, my daughter has also been able to serve on the role model side and influence some younger girls through babysitting, mission trips, and a summer camp where she worked. Whether she is the babysitter or the fun camp counselor, mentoring is taking place all the same. By having little eyes looking up to her, she is mindful of the influence she can have on their lives and careful to live in such a way as to bring glory to God.

While the antics of those in Hollywood may leave us with the impression that virtuous role models are in short supply, I want to encourage you that they are out there. Maybe not in Hollywood, but there are virtuous role models in our families, churches, Christian organizations, and other places where godly women are likely to gather. Our job is to find them and expose our daughters to these fabulous women as much as possible. In the end the ultimate role model when it comes to virtue is the author of virtue. Our daughters are more likely to look to Christ as the ultimate example if they witness mom doing so.

A New, Improved Virtuous Standard

Proverbs 31:10 opens with, "Who can find a virtuous woman? for her price is far above rubies" (KJV). Apparently, the shortage of good girls can be traced back to the Old Testament days. It is speculated that King Lemuel wrote the Proverbs 31 passage as he reflected on his mother's teaching regarding the type of wife he should seek. Theologians believe that the poem did not originate with King Lemuel's mother but was rather, a freestanding poem that had been passed down for many generations for the purpose of aiding men in identifying an ideal wife, as well as giving women a formula for becoming a virtuous woman. The twenty-two verses are in an acrostic format with each verse beginning with consecutive letters of the Hebrew alphabet to aid in easy memorization. While at first glance the virtuous woman of Proverbs 31 may appear to be an outdated fixture of the past, her character qualities stand the test of time.

The passage is just as meaningful today as it was when it was originally written. Second Timothy 3:16 reminds us that "all Scripture is God-breathed and is useful for teaching, rebuking, correcting and training in righteousness." In the remaining two chapters, we will draw from the Proverbs 31 passage the formula for raising a virtuous young woman. So often we think of the Proverbs 31 passage as being relevant only to older women, especially if your initial exposure was in the formal King James Version. In reality, virtue is something that is acquired over time. It is a pursuit that begins when our daughters are young and continues throughout a lifetime. As we take a closer look at the recipe for raising virtuous daughters, keep in mind that it will be impossible to impart these truths to our girls unless we first own them for ourselves. While that may sound like a tall order, let's remember that we are each a work in progress. As Paul and Timothy reminded the saints in Philippi, "In all my prayers for all of you, I always pray with joy because of your partnership in the gospel from the first day until now, being confident of this, that he who began a good work in you will carry it on to completion until the day of Christ Jesus" (Phil. 1:4–6). Now we know where the phrase "Be patient; God isn't finished with me yet" originated!

CHAPTER EIGHTEEN

Princess Today,

Royal Pain Tomorrow?

Imagine your little princess celebrating her initiation into the teen years at a fine restaurant with a few friends. Certainly nothing unusual, but here's where the birthday party takes a twist from the standard chorus of "Happy Birthday" sung by a sea of waiters who circle up and present the chocolate molten brownie explosion with eight forks. The real birthday treat has yet to come. When your daughter and her friends finish the dessert and exit the restaurant, a throng of paparazzi awaits them. Cameras begin flashing from every direction as they yell out to your daughter by her first name. Stunned at first, she can hardly hear their questions above the constant clicking of their cameras as they take a rapid-fire series of pictures. "You girls look beautiful!" "Where are you going?" "How does it feel to be a teenager?" As your daughter and her friends make their way down the sidewalk to the car, a curious crowd begins to gather, and some ask members of the paparazzi, "Who is she?" They repeat back your daughter's first name with a confident tone that implies that no other information should be necessary to identify this star. As the crowd of onlookers swells, many pull out their camera phones and begin taking pictures of your daughter and asking for her autograph. Your daughter takes it all in stride, stopping to sign a few autographs as the paparazzi continue snapping pictures, following her in hot pursuit. Finally, she and her friends reach the car and are quickly ushered inside while the paparazzi and curious bystanders continue to snap pictures as you drive away.

Sound outrageous? Believe it or not, scenes similar to this one are playing out all around the country. For about $250 you can hire a group of paparazzi to stalk someone of your choosing for about half an hour. Whether the occasion is a birthday party, wedding reception, graduation ceremony, or simply a much-needed boost to someone's esteem, anyone can be a celeb for a day. Or rather thirty minutes. If you want it to last a day, you have to shell out about $1,500. And to think that all I got when I turned thirteen was a measly pizza party and sleepover. As I read about this new phenomenon in a *Time* magazine article, I was struck by the fact that the almighty worship of self has become not only acceptable but epidemic. Josh Gamson, a University of San Francisco professor of sociology who studies culture and mass media, was quoted in the article as saying, "If you don't have people asking who you are, you're nobody."[1] Wow, I guess I need to give one of the paparazzi services a call so I can pay to have absolute strangers take my picture in an effort to attract other absolute strangers, who then ask who I am. Gee, that should make me feel like a "somebody." Has the need for attention reached such a level that some are willing to pay for it?

All about Me, Myself, and I

While it's reasonable to engage in an occasional narcissistic indulgence, for some the indulgence of self becomes a year-round lifestyle. Take, for example, a recent study that found college students are more narcissistic and self-centered than ever before. Five psychologists examined the responses of 16,475 college students nationwide who completed an evaluation called the Narcissistic Personality Inventory between 1982 and 2006 and asked for responses to such statements as "If I ruled the world, it would be a better place," "I think I am a special person," and "I can live my life any way I choose." By 2006 the researchers found that two-thirds of the students had above-average scores, 30 percent more than in 1982.[2]

The study's lead author, Professor Jean Twenge of San Diego State University said, "We need to stop endlessly repeating 'You're special' and having children repeat that back. . . . Kids are self-centered enough already."[3] The researchers attribute the upsurge in narcissism to the self-esteem movement that took root in the 1980s and further suggest that the effort to build self-confidence has gone too far. Twenge, the author of *Generation Me: Why Today's Young Americans Are More Confident, Assertive, Entitled—and More Miserable Than Ever Before*, said narcissists tend to lack empathy, react aggressively to criticism, and favor self-promotion over helping others. Not surprisingly, when asked to identify possible remedies to the growing problem, the researchers stated that "permissiveness seems to be a component" and that possible antidotes might include more "authoritative parenting" and "less indulgence."[4] It appears that narcissists are made rather than born.

Generation Diva

If you have a daughter, you have likely been caught up to some degree in the princess movement. I know I have. This generation of divas-in-the-making has grown up wearing Onesies announcing their "Princess" status in rhinestones. The Disney princess empire banks around $4 billion annually.[5] More likely than not, most of us have supported that fund to some degree. But not everyone thinks it's healthy to feed into the princess mentality when it comes to raising our daughters. Peggy Orenstein, an author who commonly writes on women's issues, questions whether perfect-looking princesses are really good role models for girls, claiming that we need to expose them to reality, not fantasy.[6] While I disagree on some level and see no harm in allowing our daughters to partake in the princess craze in small doses, I do feel it's possible to go overboard and create a self-indulgent royal pain in the end.

> This generation of divas-in-the-making has grown up wearing Onesies announcing their "Princess" status in rhinestones.

David Abrams, a psychotherapist and licensed professional counselor, worries that the diva influence could lead to a sense of entitlement and that girls treated like divas, or temperamental superstars, could come to believe they deserve such catering throughout their lives.[7] I'm willing to bet that each one of us, upon reading that statement, can think of countless real-life examples of girls who have been coddled to such an unhealthy degree that they have morphed into a royal terror. Trust me, you don't have to have the wealth of the Hilton family to produce a Paris Hilton attitude in your child.

"If you think about it, the more we watch TV or watch things, it's always pushing to be happy," Abrams said. "You can't be happy driving a Honda. You have to have a Mercedes." Abrams further noted that the more people look outside themselves for happiness, the less happy they'll be. "There will always be a nicer car, a bigger house and a cooler Sweet Sixteen party."[8] This trend is especially frightening when you consider that much of a child's personality is developed by the age of five and their identity is molded by the messages they receive from those closest to them.

So what's the balance when it comes to sending the message to our daughters that they are princesses? Does this mean you need to cancel your daughter's upcoming Cinderella party? Do you give her fairy godmother the night off and dress your little Cinderella in her preball garb, powder her little face with a few soot streaks, and hand her a broom? That ought to get the message across. Seriously, there is nothing wrong with indulging your daughter in a little princess treatment as long as you are sending a balanced and, better yet, biblical message.

A Proverbs 31 Princess

By looking to Proverbs 31, we see an idea of the type of woman (young and old) who is esteemed in the eyes of God. Her affinity for fine linen and purple (a color often associated with royalty) hints that she may have had a little princess in her. However, when you take a closer look at the Proverbs 31 passage, two qualities emerge that fly in the face of the princess mentality. Rather than tell you straight out what those qualities are, let me show you some key verses and see if you can recognize them. As you are reading the following verses, what quality comes to mind?

Proverbs 31:10–31

- "She selects wool and flax and works with eager hands" (v. 13).

- "She is like the merchant ships, bringing her food from afar" (v. 14).
- "She considers a field and buys it; out of her earnings she plants a vineyard" (v. 16).
- "She sets about her work vigorously; her arms are strong for her tasks" (v. 17).
- "She sees that her trading is profitable, and her lamp does not go out at night" (v. 18).
- "In her hand she holds the distaff and grasps the spindle with her fingers" (v. 19).
- "She makes coverings for her bed; she is clothed in fine linen and purple" (v. 22).
- "She makes linen garments and sells them, and supplies the merchants with sashes" (v. 24).

Needless to say, *entitlement* was not a word in the virtuous woman's vocabulary. Clothed in fine linen or not, this woman was a hard worker who was far more likely to have dirt under her nails than a tiara propped on her head. Let's stop for a minute and examine some tangible ways we can instill the value of hard work within our daughters.

First, we can put our daughters to work around the house and give them regular, age-appropriate chores. My husband has done an outstanding job of training all three of our children when it comes to helping out around the house. From the time they were very young, they have had jobs assigned to them that matched their age level and ability. From about the age of eight, they have been responsible for doing their own laundry. If they run out of clean clothes, they have no one to blame but themselves. In addition, they take rotations doing the dishes and some of the yard work. I honestly cannot remember the last time I even did the dishes and dread the day my youngest child leaves for college!

In addition, we also require each of our children to hold a job in the summer beginning at the age of sixteen. They are also responsible for depositing their paychecks and keeping track of their balance. Some of the money they earn from working is put aside in a savings account, another 10 percent is taken out (by them) for a tithe at church, and the rest can be used at their discretion for clothing, electronics, movies, and other outside leisure activities. Once they are in college, they are required to put aside some of their summer earnings to go toward some of their college expenses such as books or outside activities.

No doubt, my children have been extremely blessed and their workload cannot begin to compare to those who carry the entire financial burden to put themselves through college (many while holding full-time jobs) or go to work to help supplement the family income. Hopefully, at least, we have provided them with a baseline appreciation of the value of hard work that they will carry over into their adult years.

Take a look at some other verses in the Proverbs 31 passage and see if you can recognize another critical quality in raising a virtuous young woman.

- "Her husband has full confidence in her and lacks nothing of value" (v. 11).
- "She brings him good, not harm, all the days of her life" (v. 12).
- "She gets up while it is still dark; she provides food for her family and portions for her servant girls" (v. 15).
- "She opens her arms to the poor and extends her hands to the needy" (v. 20).
- "When it snows, she has no fear for her household; for all of them are clothed in scarlet" (v. 21).

• "She watches over the affairs of her household and does not eat the bread of idleness" (v. 27).

Again, the verses hardly point to a self-indulgent princess who puts her own needs or desires before everyone else. Ironically, the description of the virtuous woman is the antithesis of the princess attitude our culture breeds today. Children, adolescents, and teens are already prone to think that life is all about them. Unfortunately, many will grow up and fail to shed the "it's all about me" attitude. Unless, that is, we help them do so along the way.

> Children, adolescents, and teens are already prone to think that life is all about them.

The virtuous woman of Proverbs 31 puts the needs of her family above her own needs. Some may argue that this quality will come in time, magically appearing when the husband and kids arrive on the scene. Babies certainly have a way of causing you to come to the end of yourself, however; I would believe that this task would be far easier if learned on the *front end*.

Tiara Aside

Suppose a brother or sister is without clothes and daily food. If one of you says to him, "Go, I wish you well; keep warm and well fed," but does nothing about his physical needs, what good is it? (James 2:15–16)

In Proverbs 31:2, we are told that the virtuous woman "opens her arms to the poor and extends her hands to the needy." I wonder if the Proverbs 31 woman would feel the same twinge of guilt that most of us do when we meet the gaze of the beggar at the intersection holding a cardboard "will work for food" sign. Would she dig deep in her purse or avert her eyes and wait expectantly for the light to turn green? Would she answer the pleas of every charity that called during the dinner hour or offer a polite, "We gave at the office"? Would she cheerfully write a check to the multitude of teenagers requesting assistance for their summer missions trips? What about the needy juveniles peddling gift wrap, Girl Scout cookies, and Booster Club discount cards? Did she extend her hands to every needy person and every needy cause that crossed her path?

One need not look far to find the poor and destitute. We can all reflect on times when God has placed a need in our path, and it has been clear that we are to be part of His plan in meeting the need. That is not to assume that we are called to respond to *every* need we come in contact with. If we are honest, many of us would have to admit we are nothing more than seasonal givers when it comes to extending our hands to the physically needy. Christmas is our wake-up call that sounds the alarm to the fact that there are many less fortunate than we are. When the physical needs of the poor are made public, we generally respond by rushing to fill up the food pantries, sponsoring needy families, and providing winter coats and blankets. Come December 26, we breathe a sigh of relief along with the rest of the general public, convinced that we have done our yearly good deed.

A virtuous woman is not a seasonal giver but a sees-all-year-round giver. She is aware that the poor and the destitute are unable to consign their neediness to the month of December. Consistent year-round giving is the end result of an attitude of the heart that acknowledges that our resources don't belong to us in the

Consistent year-round giving is the end result of an attitude of the heart that acknowledges that our resources don't belong to us in the first place.

first place. God has allowed us the resources, and with that blessing comes a responsibility to be good stewards with what He has entrusted to us.

While I have been diligent in modeling tithing and giving financially toward charitable causes and missions, I feel I could have done a better job in modeling to my children actual feet-on-the-ground service to the needy. Oh sure, we have participated in canned food drives and buying needed items for sponsored families at Christmas time, but if I had a chance to do it over, I would have involved my children in more service-oriented projects where they are exposed to the neediest of the needy.

As it is, my children have been involved in annual youth-sponsored projects, whether bringing socks and coats to the homeless or taking missions trips. In her junior year my daughter traveled with our youth group to a small Hispanic community near the Texas-Mexico border that exposed her to the harsh reality of how others in the world live. She helped build a playscape for the area children, build and stock a food pantry at a local church, and organize a Vacation Bible School for the area children. She worked extremely hard while there, and it afforded her the opportunity to "extend her hand to the needy." The trip fell over her spring break vacation, and weeks prior she was invited by a friend to go snow skiing. She begged and pleaded to go on the trip with her friend, but we made the tough call that she needed to fulfill her commitment to go on the mission trip. I remained home during the trip and worried that she would spend the entire time thinking about where she "could have been" or "might have been" during spring break, praying all the while that God would show her the blessing of serving others.

God answered that prayer, and when she returned, she talked nonstop about the playscape that took almost the entire week to build. Princesses need not apply for this job. She described in detail the endless loads of pea gravel hauled one wheelbarrow at a time, the parts assembled and bolted together, and then with excitement, the moment of truth. I will never forget the pride in her voice as she described the reward of seeing the children play on the playscape for the first time—many who had never even seen a playscape until the moment of the unveiling. How I wish I had involved my children sooner in the blessing of serving those less fortunate!

While in the process of writing this chapter, I took the opportunity to confess to my daughter that I have been personally convicted about my own "inner princess" that often holds me back from getting my hands dirty and feet moving when it comes to serving others. I also confessed that I fear I may have modeled to her an attitude that is "too much princess" and "too little servant." We both committed to give the matter over to the Lord and have even talked about going on a mission trip together sometime during her college years. Also, in an effort to learn to say no to ourselves when it comes to our own wants and yes to others who have true needs, we decided to sponsor a child together through Compassion International.[9] My daughter chose a little boy from Thailand, and we split the monthly sponsorship fee, which amounted to $18 for each of us. I figure I spend that much on my ridiculous grande vanilla latte habit, and she spends at least that much on her shoe habit (my fault on that one, too!). We so look forward to receiving the updates and pictures about his progress, and I often hear my daughter telling her friends about little Aphichok from Thailand and showing them his picture. Our church takes a mission trip to Thailand several times a year, and Paige and I are hoping for the opportunity to meet him someday.

Expose your daughter to the blessing of serving others in Jesus' name. If she's young, volunteer in a soup kitchen or sponsor needy families at Christmas time and take her with you to pick out the gifts. Find a mission trip that is kid friendly and take her outside her normal comfort zone. The mission trip my church makes to the Texas-Mexico border several times a year allows involvement of families with kids of all ages. Even if it is impossible for you physically to go or financially to give at this time, model the importance of praying with your daughter for those who fall into the needy category. There is nothing wrong with telling your daughter she's a princess and treating her like one on occasion. The key will be emphasizing servanthood above princess-hood. After all, tiaras were never meant to be worn full-time.

CHAPTER NINETEEN

The Timeless Qualities of a Virtuous Young Woman

O ften when speaking to teen girls, I challenge them with the question, "Are you the type of girl who has a reputation?" The question makes some of the girls fidget a bit in their seats. If you looked up the word *reputation* in the dictionary, you might find this definition: "the generally accepted estimation of somebody; character, standing, name." The truth is, each of us has a reputation, a "generally accepted estimation"

> The truth is, each of us has a reputation.

as determined by others, and that estimation can be overall good or bad. In order to illustrate the power of this "estimation" factor when determining a person's reputation, I tell the girls that I'm going to announce several well-known celebrity personalities and when I do, they should think of one or two words to describe the person (not out loud, of course). I toss out names like Britney Spears, Michael Jackson, Tom Cruise, Carrie Underwood, and The Jonas Brothers. I think you can imagine some of the words the girls come up with to describe the above personalities (in no particular order): *crazy, cute, psycho, pervert, adorable, innocent, talented, sleaze,* and the list goes on. I then tell the girls that they just branded each person with a designated reputation based on the public's "generally accepted estimation." I point out that even though they are not famous and in the public eye, they are still being "estimated" by others on a daily basis. I then challenge them to think of what one or two words others who know them might use to describe their character if asked. Certainly, it's an unsettling thought for some. I imagine I would have been among the "unsettled" had I been challenged by that thought at their age.

The Value of a Good Name

I once heard a speaker say, "You are who you've been becoming." Wow, what a powerful statement! Our girls need to know that you are judged by your actions. In my years of working with teen and college girls, I have had a fair share cry on my shoulder over actions that have left them with tainted reputations. As we discussed in Conversation 3, it is fairly common for children and teens to have a cognitive disconnect when it comes to making choices. In other words, it is difficult for them to mentally walk a decision down its logical path and weigh the possible consequences of the action in question. Most of us likely can relate to that challenge during our adolescent and teen years and have our own fair share of negative consequences we tallied up as a result.

However, this is where we must be faithful in helping our daughters see that actions determine character and character, in turn, determines reputation. In addition, we must also help them see the value that comes from the pursuit of virtue.

Proverbs 22:1 reminds us that "a good name is rather to be chosen than great riches" (KJV). Socrates, the Greek philosopher from the fourth century B.C., once said, "Regard your good name as the richest jewel that can possibly be possessed. The way to gain a good reputation is to endeavor to be what you desire to appear." Unfortunately, this counsel was too late for *American Idol* contestant Antonella Barba. In the season that this college-aged student appeared on the show, some untimely topless photos circulated the Internet and sealed her reputation. The pictures were taken "in fun" with her friends at the beach and were never meant to be shared with the public, much less the World Wide Web. Interestingly, the reputation she earned as a result of the photos did not line up with the person she "endeavored to be." In an interview with *People* magazine regarding the racy photos, she said, "Yes, it's true that my name is more well-known because of it, but I'm not known for the things that I would like to be known for right now. I wanted to make a name for myself in singing. The pictures that have been released of me . . . were very personal and that is not how I intended to portray myself. I'd rather promote myself in a more classy way."[1]

Though unfortunate for this young lady, this was a hard lesson to learn. And I must say that I was impressed with her actions that have since followed in an effort to redefine her reputation. She was

> **P**roverbs 22:1 reminds us that "a good name is rather to be chosen than great riches" (KJV).

offered six figures to host the raunchy *Girls Gone Wild* videos, but she declined. It was also rumored that *Playboy* was interested in paying her to pose nude in their magazine, but she made clear that she would not be interested. Good for her. Joseph Hall, an English bishop from the sixteenth century, once said, "A reputation once broken may possibly be repaired, but the world will always keep their eyes on the spot where the crack was." Such is the unfortunate case with Ms. Barba. Several years have passed, yet if you google her name, you will find numerous references to the scandal, including Wikipedia (online encyclopedia). And as you can imagine, the pictures are certainly here to stay. Again, she is to be applauded for making wise choices after the fact. One can only hope that with time she will be remembered for the person she has since become.

We must be faithful in sharing the key to obtaining a good reputation with our daughters. *What is the key?* you may wonder. It can be found in Proverbs 3:1–4: "My son, do not forget my teaching, but keep my commands in your heart, for they will prolong your life many years and bring you prosperity. Let love and faithfulness never leave you; bind them around your neck, write them on the tablet of your heart. Then you will win favor and a good name in the sight of God and man." In order to remember God's teaching, our daughters must first know God's teaching. Upon knowing it, they must tuck it away in their hearts and pull from that reserve when the need arises. This is the point of impact when God's standard goes beyond a simple head knowledge and takes root in the heart. We can do our part to provide them with adequate teaching over the years, but we cannot make them treasure that teaching in their hearts. Furthermore, we cannot make them draw upon those truths and apply them to their daily lives. We can, however, pray like crazy from the sidelines.

If we were to step into a time machine and take a little journey back to your high school years, what sort of girl would we find?

Better yet, what if we asked your classmates to describe that girl? I'm not talking about the outside. How do they remember the girl in the Jordache jeans with the spiral perm? Was she nice, fun, funny, or kind? Was she a devoted Christian who walked her talk? Or was she a gossipy, mean girl with loose morals? In other words, what was your *reputation*? How has the "generally accepted estimation" of you changed over the years? I would guess that most of us have changed for the better and all but for the grace of God—Amen?

Perhaps a few of us were mindful in the early years of God's standard of a godly and virtuous reputation and sought to mold our character accordingly. However, I'm willing to bet that many of us, myself included, conformed instead to the culture's standard. Even, I dare say, many who were raised in the church and were taught God's virtuous standard. I feel it's important for us to reflect back on our own growing-up journey as we raise our daughters. The key word I want us to remember is *journey*. Just as most of us experienced firsthand, conforming to God's standard will be a process that occurs over time.

Laughing at the Days to Come

Isn't it the desire of every mother to see her children live a happy life? Proverbs 31:25 reminds us that the virtuous woman was "clothed with strength and dignity" and could "laugh at the days to come." The Hebrew word for "dignity" is *hadar, (haw-dawr')*, which means "magnificence, ornament or splendor—beauty, comeliness, excellency, glorious, glory, goodly, honor, majesty."[2] Forget the tiaras and other modern-day princess accoutrements being peddled to our girls. Sounds like your princess has a better shot at finding "happily ever after" by clothing herself in none other than dignity. How many people, well-known or otherwise, can you think of who, in spite of having all the things the world claims will bring happiness (money, fame, constant attention), find themselves empty and miserable? They can't laugh at the day at hand, much less the days to come. Yet, if you take a closer look, I imagine you would find a person who worships the god of self rather than the Almighty God of this universe. Ironically, the focus on self (the created) rather than God (the Creator) leaves them empty and craving something more.

In 2004 a survey was conducted that asked a sample of Americans, "Would you say that you are very happy, pretty happy, or not too happy?" Religious people (defined as those who attend a house of worship at least once per week) were more than twice as likely as the secular (defined as those who never attend a house of worship) to say they were "very happy." Meanwhile, secular people were nearly three times as likely as the religious to say they were not too happy. In the same survey, religious people were more than a third more likely than the secular to say they were optimistic about the future.[3]

The study further notes: "The happiness gap between religious and secular people is not because of money or other personal characteristics. Imagine two people who are identical in every important way—income, education, age, sex, family status, race and political views. The only difference is that the first person is religious; the second is secular. The religious person will still be 21 percentage points more likely than the secular person to say that he or she is very happy."[4] It shouldn't come as a surprise that a secular study confirms that the happiest people on earth are those who believe in and follow God.

Consider the following verses:

How happy are those who can live in your house, always singing your praises. (Ps. 84:4 NLT)

Happy are those who are strong in the LORD, who set their minds on a pilgrimage to Jerusalem. (Ps. 84:5 NLT)

O LORD almighty, happy are those who trust in you. (Ps. 84:12 NLT)

Happy are those who hear the joyful call to worship, for they will walk in the light of your presence, LORD. (Ps. 89:15 NLT)

Happy are those whom you discipline, LORD, and those whom you teach from your law. (Ps. 94:12 NLT)

Happy are those who deal justly with others and always do what is right. (Ps. 106:3 NLT)

Praise the LORD! Happy are those who fear the LORD. Yes, happy are those who delight in doing what he commands. (Ps. 112:1 NLT)

Happy are those who obey his decrees and search for him with all their hearts. (Ps. 119:2 NLT)

How happy are those who fear the LORD—all who follow his ways! (Ps. 128:1 NLT)

Happy indeed are those whose God is the LORD. (Ps. 144:15 NLT)

But happy are those who have the God of Israel as their helper, whose hope is in the LORD their God. (Ps. 146:5 NLT)

Wisdom is a tree of life to those who embrace her; happy are those who hold her tightly. (Prov.

How happy are those who fear the LORD—all who follow his ways! (Ps. 128:1 NLT)

3:18 NLT)

Happy are those who listen to me, watching for me
daily at my gates, waiting for me outside my home!
(Prov. 8:34 NLT)

Now that's what I call a recipe for happiness! Have you passed
this family recipe down to your daughter?

A Life of Purpose

King Solomon was someone who was known for possessing great
wisdom. He had personally reaped the benefits of wealth, knowledge, and power; yet he continued to question the meaning of life.
At the end of Ecclesiastes he concluded with this: "Now all has been
heard; here is the conclusion of the matter: Fear God and keep his
commandments, for this is the whole duty of man" (Eccl. 12:13).

The Proverbs 31 woman's ability to "fear the Lord" was a key
factor in her being set apart from other women. Verse 30 reminds
us that "charm is deceptive, and beauty is fleeting; but a woman
who fears the LORD is to be praised." If we are to become virtuous,
we too, must come to this same conclusion. We must set out to
discover what, exactly, it means to fear the Lord. And we must in
turn pass this timeless quality on to our daughters. The Bible men-
tions several types of fear, so we need to understand the type of fear
spoken of in the phrase "fear of the Lord." At first glance, we might
wonder if the fear of the Lord is the same type of fear we are most
accustomed to experiencing, one best equated with being "afraid."

The *Holman Illustrated Bible Dictionary* describes secular fear as
the natural feeling of alarm caused by the expectation of imminent
danger, pain, or disaster while religious fear appears as the result of
awe and reverence toward a supreme power. It goes on to say that
this sense of fear comes as individuals encounter the divine in the

context of revelation. When God appears to a person, the person experiences the reality of God's holiness. This self-disclosure of God points to the vast distinction between humans and God, to the mysterious characteristic of God that at the same time attracts and repels. A mystery in divine holiness causes individuals to become overwhelmed with a sense of awe and fear. It further concludes that the fear of God is not to be understood as the dread that comes out of fear of punishment, but as the reverential regard and the awe that comes out of recognition and submission to the divine. It is the revelation of God's will to which the believer submits in obedience.[5]

New Unger's Bible Dictionary describes fear of the Lord as something that:

- Dreads God's displeasure.
- Desires God's favor.
- Reveres God's holiness.
- Submits cheerfully to God's will.
- Is grateful for God's benefits.
- Sincerely worships God.
- Conscientiously obeys God's commandments.[6]

It also states that fear and love must coexist in us before we can please and rightly serve God. Apparently God knew we would need to possess a godly fear before we could adequately grasp His heavenly love. The Proverbs 31 woman clearly had learned to fear the Lord and, as a result, served Him faithfully and wholeheartedly. No doubt, she had been set apart and Proverbs 31:29 records her legacy that "many women do noble things, but you surpass them all." It will be impossible for our daughters to live a life of purpose apart from developing a healthy "fear of the Lord." It is not surprising that fear of the Lord is the critical component that sets the virtuous woman apart from other women. A woman who fears the Lord has made the Lord the *foundation* of her life. A life lived in purpose is a life lived in awe and reverence of a Holy God. Pure and simple.

Final Thoughts

I can't think of a better way to end this book than with a reminder about the timeless qualities of a virtuous woman. Amazingly, every one of the conversations addressed in this book is built upon an underlying foundation of godly virtue. When I became a Christian at the age of twenty-one, *virtue* was not a word in my vocabulary. I was your typical girl who bought the lies of the culture and suffered plenty of fallout along the way. No doubt, it would have taken several U-haul trucks to haul my sins to the foot of the cross, but fortunately Jesus did the dirty work for me. God, in His mercy had forgiven my sins, and behold, I became a new creation (see 2 Cor. 5:17).

In the days that followed my conversion to Christianity, I felt like a wrecking ball had been released and the flimsy structure my life had previously been built on came crumbling to the ground in a pile of dusty ashes and debris. God took one look at my old life and deemed it uninhabitable. With the care of a master architect, He laid a new foundation and the rebuilding process began. In truth, it would take nearly a decade to repair the damage sustained from twenty-one years of believing the lies. One board, one nail, one brick at a time, God helped me replace each lie with His amazing truth.

Two years after becoming a Christian (which marked the demolition of my old life), I had my first child (a son) and within four years, I had my second (a daughter). My third child (a son) followed a couple of years later. I share that detail to say that my life was still very much in the rebuilding phase during my children's most impressionable years. You can't raze a structure and rebuild in a day, so needless to say, my early parenting years were when my own heart was under construction. And at the time, the thought certainly crossed my mind: *How can I raise a daughter who resists the lies of the culture and builds a foundation on God's truths when I am still teetering on wobbly scaffolding, caulking the cracks of my own life?* Of course, there was only one way. I would need God's help.

If you are feeling overwhelmed and grossly under qualified with the task at hand, I want to encourage you. God can work His good in any situation if given the opportunity and I am living proof of that promise. The mother I am to my now, eighteen-year-old daughter is not the mother I was when she was two, five, ten, or fourteen. And the mother I am today, though much improved, is still desperately dependent on the Lord to take up the slack for my shortcomings. I don't know where you are in the parenting journey, but I want to remind you to be easy on yourself. None of us has it all together—even those of us writing the parenting books! You will make mistakes along the way. I know I did. You will second-guess decisions you have made. I know I did. And as I mentioned in the introduction of this book, you will always wonder if you're doing enough. When that happens, remind yourself that God is sufficient. As much as you love your daughter and want to see her fall madly in love with Jesus and live a life devoted to Him, God loves her all the more and wants the same things for her.

I can't make any guarantees that reading this book and implementing the principles herein will produce the end result of a daughter who embraces God's truths and rejects the culture's lies. But I can tell you this: If you practice the principles contained on these pages and lean on the Lord for wisdom, strength, and discernment, you will have *provided your daughter with the tools* to embrace God's truths and reject the culture's lies. You can't force her to build her life on God's truths—she will have to make that decision on her own. I began this book (in the introduction) with a statement that bears repeating: God is not looking for perfect mothers to raise perfect daughters. He's looking for imperfect mothers who are raising imperfect daughters in an imperfect world, and desperately dependant on a perfect God for the results.

> But he said to me, "My grace is sufficient for you,
> for my power is made perfect in weakness." Therefore I will
> boast all the more gladly about my weaknesses, so that
> Christ's power may rest on me. (2 Cor. 12:9)

Appendix

My Child, Do You Remember Me?

My child, do you remember me?
We met so long ago.
You were formed inside my womb
Yet never allowed to grow.

I never got to see your face
Or hold you in my arms.
I pray someday you'll understand;
I never meant you harm.

I missed playing peekaboo
And going to the park.
I missed holding you in my lap
When you were afraid of the dark.

I missed your pretty pictures
Of rainbows in the sky.
I missed the cards on Mother's Day,
The kind that make you cry.

I missed your learning to ride a bike
And your first dive into the pool.
I missed your every summertime
And your every first day of school.

I missed your every birthday
And watching you grow each year.
I missed saying, "I love you,"
And showing how much I care.

My child, will you forgive me
For the life I stole from you?
Will you know the tears I've shed
For that child I never knew?

I know you're in a better place,
And someday I'll meet you there.
For Jesus has forgiven me,
My sin I no longer bear.

My child, will you remember me
On that day we meet again?
Will you even know my face
Or wonder where I've been?

"Yes Mother, I remember you;
We met so long ago.
Why I could not stay with you
I really do not know."

"Come with me and meet the Lord,"
My child will smile and say.
"I'll take your hand and lead you there,
For He'll wash your tears away."

Finally, I'll approach His throne,
My sins as white as snow,
And He'll hold me tight and say to me,
"My child, welcome home."

© Vicki Courtney

Notes

Chapter 1

1. Satkar Gidda, "Attracting Consumers through Package and Product Innovation," May 23, 2005; www.brandchannel.com/brand_speak. asp?bs_id=111.

2. Anastasia Goodstein, "What Can Industry Do to Stop the Onslaught?" *The Huffington Post*, October 2, 2007, www.huffington post.com/anastasia-goodstein/what-can-industry-do-to-s_b_66798.html.

3. Ibid.

4. Anne Becker, "MTV VMAs Ratings, Web Traffic Up Video Music Awards Move to Las Vegas, Only Air Once," Broadcasting & Cable, September 10, 2007, www.broadcastingcable.com/article/CA6477262. html?rssid=193.

5. "Nicole Richie Transitions to MILF," www.tmz.com/2008/02/11/nicole-richie-transitions-to-milf.

6. Joan Jacobs Brumberg, *The Body Project: An Intimate History of American Girls* (1998), xxi.

7. Ibid., xx.

8. The Dove Foundation, www.campaignforrealbeauty.com/press. asp?section=news&id=110.

9. Brumberg, *The Body Project*, 66.

10. Ibid., 70.

11. Ibid., 107, picture 25.

Chapter 2

1. Brumberg, *The Body Project*, xxiv.

2. "Fashion Designers Still Blind to Reality," February 23, 2006, www. aphroditewomenshealth.com/news/20060123003254_health_news.shtml.

3. See www.pediatrics.about.com/cs/growthcharts2/f/avg_ht_ female.htm.

4. "Fashion Designers Still Blind to Reality."

5. Brumberg, *The Body Project*, 110.

6. See www.pediatrics.about.com/cs/growthcharts2/f/avg_wt_ female.htm.

7. Ibid., 119.

8. Mary Pipher, *Reviving Ophelia: Saving the Selves of Adolescent Girls* (New York: Ballantine Books, 1994).

9. Walt Mueller, "Mirror Mirror," www.cpyu.org/Page.aspx?id= 233021.

10. Nancy Etcoff, Susie Orbach, Jennifer Scott, and Heidi D'Agostino, "The Real Truth about Beauty: A Global Report—Findings of the Global Study on Women, Beauty, and Well-Being," commissioned by Dove, September 2004, www.campaignforrealbeauty.com/press. asp?section=news&id=110.

11. Pam DeFiglio, "Teen Girls Skeptical about Making Peace with Their Bodies," *Seventeen*, November 5, 2007, www.dailyherald.com/ story/?id=69540.

12. Ginny Olson, *Teenage Girls: Exploring Issues Adolescent Girls Face and Strategies to Help Them* (Grand Rapids, MI: Zondervan, 2006).

13. Ibid.

14. Joan Jacobs Brumberg, *Fasting Girls: The Emergence of Anorexia Nervosa as a Modern Disease* (Cambridge, Mass.: Harvard University Press, 1988).

15. Kim Chernin, *The Hungry Self: Women, Eating, and Identity* (New York: Times Books, 1985).

16. U.S. Department for Heath and Human Services, "Children and Teens Told by Doctors that They Were Overweight—United States, 1999–2002," *Morbidity & Mortality Weekly Report* 54, no. 34 (September 2, 2005): 848–49.

17. Ibid., 236.

18. See www.blogcritics.org/archives/2007/02/02/202514.php.

19. The National Center on Addiction and Substance Abuse (CASA) at Columbia University, *Food for Thought: Substance Abuse and Eating Disorder* (New York: CASA, December 2003), ii, www.casacolumbia.org/pdshopprov/files/food_for_thought_12_03.pdf.

20. Lisa Berzins, "Dying to be thin: the prevention of eating disorders and the role of federal policy. APA co-sponsored congressional briefing," USA. November 1997.

21. Olson, *Teenage Girls*, 55–56.

22. J. A. O'Dea and S. Abraham, "Association Between Self-Concept and Body Weight, Gender, and Pubertal Development Among Male and Female Adolescents," *Adolescence* 34 (Spring 1999): 69–79.

23. Sarah Baicker, "For teens, obesity no laughing matter," October 23, 2007. According to new research from the University of Minnesota; Dianne Neumark-Sztainer, the study's lead researcher, tracked 2,500 adolescents over five years, news.medill.northwestern.edu/washington/news.aspx?id=66261.

24. Ibid.

25. See www.tmz.com/2007/10/24/haydens-cottage-cheese-thighs-fact-or-fiction.

26. See beauty.ivillage.com/skinbody/cellulite/0,,newbeauty_8ht9nz41,00.html; www.vanguardngr.com/articles/2002/features/fashion/fas223072006.html.

27. Ibid.

28. Ibid.

29. Ibid.

Chapter 3

1. "Sexualization of Girls is Linked to Common Mental Health Problems in Girls and Women—Eating Disorders, Low Self-Esteem, and Depression," February 19, 2007, www.apa.org/releases/sexualization.html.

2. Ibid.

3. Cited in Ginny Olson, *Teenage Girls: Exploring Issues Adolescent Girls Face and Strategies to Help Them*, from A. E. Field et al., "Exposure to the Mass Media and Weight Concerns Among Girls," *Pediatrics* 103 (March 1999). Cited in Marjorie Hogan, "Media Education Offers Help on Children's Body Image Problems," AAP News, May 1999, www.aap.org/advocacy/hogan599.htm; accessed December 18, 2005.

4. Ibid.

5. See www.cjonline.com/stories/010207/tee_dieting.shtml, citing a study in *Pediatrics*, January.

6. Information based on author's observation.

7. See www.washingtonpost.com/wp-dyn/content/article/2007/02/16/AR2007021602263_pf.html.

8. APA study; *(Frederickson & Roberts, 1997; McKinley & Hyde, 1996).*

9. Shaunti Feldhahn and Lisa Rice, *For Young Women Only: What You Need to Know about How Guys Think* (Sisters, OR: Multnomah, 2006).

10. See www.jezebel.com/gossip/photoshop-of-horrors/heres-our-winner-redbook-shatters-our-faith-in-well-not-publishing-but-maybe-god-278919.php.

11. Naomi Wolf, *The Beauty Myth: How Images of Beauty are Used Against Women* (New York: Harper Perennial, 2002). I do not endorse this book as a whole and disagree wholeheartedly with the author's radical feminist view and negative view of Christianity, but found some of the research to be useful in citing the media's damage when it comes to the "beauty myth."

12. "Effects of Aging on Your Body," www.cnn.com/2007/HEALTH/07/27/life.stages/index.html, accessed August 14, 2007.

Chapter 4

1. "Only Two Percent of Women Describe Themselves as Beautiful; New Global Study Uncovers Desire for Broader Definition of Beauty,"

September 29, 2004, www.campaignforrealbeauty.com/press.asp?
section=news&id=110.

2. Ibid.

Chapter 5

1. A link to the software I use can be found at www.vickicourtney.
com/books_resources.htm.

2. Victoria Stagg Elliott, "Health risks make some fashions 'don'ts,'"
www.ama-assn.org/amednews/2002/08/05/hlsc0805.htm. Physicians say
style trends can cause infections, damage the musculoskeletal system,
and impact fertility.

3. Mary Jane Minkin, "The Lowdown on Thongs; Are panties a
health risk?," www.prevention.com/cda/article/the-lowdown-
onthongs/5f8966263d803110VgnVCM20000012281eac____/health/
health.experts/mary.jane.minkin.md.

4. "Tattoos and Piercings: What to Know Beforehand," www.mayo
clinic.com/health/tattoos-and-piercings/MC00020.

5. Ibid.

6. Ibid.

7. C. S. Lewis, *The Last Battle* (New York: HarperCollins Publishers,
1956).

Chapter 6

1. Terri Apter, *You Don't Really Know Me: Why Mothers and
Daughters Fight and How Both Can Win* (Boston, MA: W. W. Norton
& Co., 2004), 33, cited in Ginny Olson; *Teenage Girls: Exploring Issues
Adolescent Girls Face and Strategies to Help Them*; 166.

2. Peter Bearman and Hannah Bruchner, et al, "Peer Potential:
Making the Most of How Teens Influence Each Other," www.teen
pregnancy.org, cited in Anita M. Smith, "The Power of Peers," www.
youthdevelopment.org/articles/fp109901.htm.

3. Ibid.

4. Ibid.

5. Ibid.

6. Ibid.

Chapter 7

1. This June 2006 study was conducted by Margaret Blythe, M.D., and her colleagues at Indiana University Medical Center. *Archives of Pediatrics and Adolescent Medicine* is one of the JAMA Archives journals. According to a study done by the National Campaign to Prevent Teen Pregnancy in 2004, two-thirds of all sexually experienced teens said they wished they had waited longer before having sex. (In studies in both 2004 and 2004, the number of girls who regretted sex was consistently higher than the number of boys.)

2. Survey of 1,000 girls conducted by Emory University, http://acgreen.com/default.aspx?sectionid=2456&pageid5330; AC Green Youth Foundation.

3. Jeannette Walls, "Jessica photos too steamy for her mom; Simpson parents don't seem to agree on their daughter's look" August 8, 2006, www.msnbc.msn.com/id/13639810.

4. Joan Jacobs Brumberg, *The Body Project*.

5. Francine Benton, *Etiquette: The Complete Guide for Day-to-Day Living the Correct Way* (New York: Random House, 1956).

6. Melissa Trevathan and Sissy Goff, *All You Need to Know about Raising Girls* (Grand Rapids, MI: Zondervan, 2007), 162.

7. Ibid.

Chapter 8

1. Dawn Eden, *The Thrill of the Chaste: Finding Fulfillment While Keeping Your Clothes On*, 17.

2. Bella English, "Countering Hypersexualized Marketing Aimed at Young Girls," *Boston Globe*, March 12, 2005, quoted in Wendy Shalit, *Girls Gone Mild*, 10.

3. W. D. Mosher, A. Chandra, J. Jones, "Sexual Behavior and Selected Health Measures: Men and Women 15–44 Years of Age, United States; 2002," *Advance Data from Vital and Health Statistics, a publication of the Centers for Disease Control*, no. 362 (September 15, 2005), quoted in Ginny Olson, *Teenage Girls: Exploring Issues Adolescent Girls Face and Strategies to Help Them*.

4. "Youth Risk Behavior Surveillance System—National College Health Risk Behavior Survey, 1995."

5. See www.washingtonpost.com/wp-dyn/content/article/2006/12/19/AR2006121901274.html. Wait Until Marriage? 'Extremely Challenging'; Wednesday, December 20, 2006; Page A02; January issue of Public Health Reports; National Survey of Family Growth Lawrence B. Finer of the Guttmacher Institute, the study's author.

6. POLL: American Sex Survey. A Peek Beneath the Sheets; analysis by Gary Langer, with Cheryl Arnedt and Dalia Sussman; October 21, 2004, abcnews.go.com/Primetime/PollVault/story?id=156921&page=1.

7. Ibid.

Chapter 9

1. David Larson and Mary Ann Mayo, "Believe Well, Live Well," Family Research Council (1994).

2. David B. Larson, M.D., NMSPH, et al, "The Costly Consequences of Divorce: Assessing the Clinical, Economic, and Public Health Impact of Marital Disruption in the United States," National Institute for Healthcare Research, Rockville, Maryland, (1994): 84–85.

3. Ibid.

4. 1995 National Survey of Family Growth. National Center for Health Statistics. "Cycle 5: Public Use Date Files, Codebooks and Documentation," available at cdc.gov/nchs/about/major/nsfg/nsfg 1-5doc_5.htm.

5. Wendy Shalit, *Girls Gone Mild*, Data from National Longitudinal Study of Youth from 1979 to 2000. This study of more than seven thousand men and women (at age eighteen and again at age thirty-eight) found that individuals who were abstinent until marriage had only half the risk of divorce of nonabstinent. Couples who saved sex for their wedding night have a divorce rate three times lower than that of other couples, 64.

6. In a study of 279 female adolescents published in the *Archives of Pediatrics and Adolescent Medicine* in June 2006, about 41 percent of girls ages fourteen to seventeen reported having "unwanted sex." Most of the girls had "unwanted sex because they feared the partner would get angry if denied sex."

7. National Campaign to Prevent Teen Pregnancy, 2004.

8. Dawn Eden, *The Thrill of the Chaste: Finding Fulfillment While Keeping Your Clothes On* (Nashville: Thomas Nelson, 2006), 35.

9. Yvonne K. Fulbright, "Friends with Benefits a Bum Deal?" December 4, 2007. www.foxnews.com/story/0,2933,314943,00.html.

10. Ibid.

11. Ibid.

12. Independent Women's Forum study "Hooking Up, Hanging Out, and Hoping for Mr. Right."

13. Ibid.

14. Ginny Olson, *Teenage Girls: Exploring Issues Adolescent Girls Face and Strategies to Help Them.*

15. Dear Abby found in *The Austin American Statesman.*

16. *Seventeen*, January 2003, 115.

17. K. Christensson et al., "Effect of Nipple Stimulation on Uterine Activity and on Plasma Levels of Oxytocin in Full Term, Healthy, Pregnant Women," *Acta Obstetricia et Gynecologica Scandinavia* 68 (1989): 205–10; Larry J. Young and Zuoxin Wang, "The Neurobiology of Pair Bonding," *Nature Neuroscience* 7, no. 10 (October 2004): 1048–54; K. M. Kendrick, "Oxytocin, Motherhood, and Bonding," *Experimental Physiology* 85 (March 2000): 111S–124S, cited in "Unprotected: A Campus Psychiatrist Reveals How Political Correctness in Her Profession Endangers Every Student."

18. Anonymous, M.D, *Unprotected: A Campus Psychiatrist Reveals How Political Correctness in Her Profession Endangers Every Student.*

19. Michael Kosfeld, et al., "Oxytocin Increases Trust in Humans," *Nature* 435 (June 2005): 673.

20. "The Benefits of Chastity Before Marriage," www.foreverfamilies.net/xml/articles/benefitsofchastity.aspx.

21. Dawn Eden, *The Thrill of the Chaste: Finding Fulfillment While Keeping Your Clothes On*, 32–33.

22. Wendy Shalit, *Girls Gone Mild*, The National Longitudinal Survey of Adolescent Health, Wave II (1996).

23. Robert E. Rector, Kirk A. Johnson, and Lauren R. Noyes, "Sexually Active Teenagers Are More Likely to Be Depressed and to Attempt Suicide," Heritage Center for Data Analysis, 2003, www.heritage.org.

24. K. Joyner and R. Udry, "You Don't Bring Me Anything but Down: Adolescent Romance and Depression," *Journal of Health and Social Behavior* 41, no. 4 (December 2000): 369–91, cited in *Unprotected: A Campus Psychiatrist Reveals How Political Correctness in Her Profession Endangers Every Student*, Anonymous, M.D. See also Deeanna Franklin, "Romantic Stress Tied to Depression in Sensitive Girls," *Clinical Psychiatric News*, April 2005, 31; and Denise D. Hallfors et al., "Which Comes First in Adolescence—Sex and Drugs or Depression?" *American Journal of Preventive Medicine* 29, no. 3 (2005): 163–70.

25. CDC (2008). Nationally Represented CDC Study Finds 1 in 4 Teenage Girls has a Sexually Transmitted Disease, March 11, 1008 Press release, www.cdc.gov/std conference/2008/media/release-11March2008. htm.

26. See www.cdc.gov/std/hpv/default.htm.

27. See www.cdc.gov/std/chlamydia/default.htm.

28. See www.cdc.gov/od/oc/media/pressrel/r050712.htm. The findings were based on responses from participants in the National Health and Nutrition Examination Survey (NHANES) from 1999 to 2002 (Abstract TP-078).

29. Anonymous, M.D., *Unprotected: A Campus Psychiatrist Reveals How Political Correctness in Her Profession Endangers Every Student*, 118.

30. Ibid., 110.

31. Maryann Leslie and Richard St. Pierre, "Osteoporosis: Implications for Risk Reduction in the College Setting," *Journal of American College Health* 48 (September 1999), 114–15.

32. Ibid., 115.

Chapter 10

1. See www.answers.com/topic/risk-behaviors-teen-pregnancy.

2. Ibid.

3. Alan Guttmacher Institute Web site, www.agi-usa.org.

4. Ibid.

5. See www.afterabortion.com.

6. "Teen births up for first time in 15 years," December 5, 2007, www.cnn.com/2007/HEALTH/12/05/teen.births.ap/index.html.

7. National Campaign to Prevent Teen Pregnancy. *With One Voice 2004: America's Adults and Teens Sound Off about Teen Pregnancy* (December 2004).

8. National Committee for Adoption. *Adoption Factbook: U.S. Data, Issues, Regulations, and Resources* (Washington, D.C.: National Committee for Adoption, 1989).

9. Cheryl D. Hayes, ed., *Risking the Future: Adolescent Sexuality, Pregnancy and Childbearing* (Washington, D.C.: National Academy Press, 1987).

10. Ibid.

11. March of Dimes—Birth Defects Foundation. P.O. 1657, Wilkes-Barre, PA. 18703, 19 May 1994.

12. Kids Count Missouri, www.oseda.missouri.edu.

13. Campaign for Our Children, www.cfoc.org/statscost.html.

14. Margery Eagan, "Single mom's the word; Mag makes role models out of unwed celebs with babies," November 29, 2007, www.news.bostonherald.com/news/opinion/columnists/view.bg?articleid=1047741.

15. Eric Aasen, "Rising numbers, Hollywood put spotlight on teen pregnancy," January 26, 2008, *The Dallas Morning News*, www.dallasnews.com/sharedcontent/dws/dn/latestnews/stories/012708dnmetteenmoms.a983de.html.

16. Technical Analysis Paper No. 42, U.S. Department of Health and Human Services, Office of Income.

Chapter 11

1. Hanna Rosin, "Even Evangelical Teens Do It: How Religious Beliefs Do and Don't Influence Sexual Behavior," May 30, 2007, www.slate.com/id/2167293, from Mark Regnerus, *Forbidden Fruit: Sex & Religion in the Lives of American Teenagers* (Oxford University Press, 2007). The book is a serious work of sociology based on several comprehensive surveys of young adults, coupled with in-depth interviews.

2. Ibid.

3. Diana Jean Schemo, "Mothers of Sex-Active Youths Often Think They're Virgins," *The New York Times*, www.nytimes.com/2002/09/05/national/05SEX.html.

4. Hanna Rosin, "Even Evangelical Teens Do It," www.slate.com/id/2167293.

5. Ibid.

6. "Taking the Pledge," May 22, 2005, www.cbsnews.com/stories/2005/05/20/60minutes/main696975_page2.shtml.

7. Ibid.

8. The Heritage Foundation, "Abstinence Statistics & Studies: Teen Virginity Pledges Lead to Better Life Outcomes, Study Finds," September 21, 2004, www.abstinence.net/library/index.php?entryid=1396.

9. Ibid.

10. Joan Jacobs Brumberg, *The Body Project*, 4–5.

11. Joan Jacobs Brumberg, *The Body Project*, "Studies of risky behavior in adolescence reveal that boys and girls from all social classes experience a lag between the body's capability and the mind's capacity to comprehend the consequences of sex. In other words: adolescents are capable of reproduction, and they display sexual interest, before their minds are able to do the kind of reasoning necessary for the long-term, hypothetical planning that sexuality requires (How would I care for a baby? What would we do if I became pregnant?)," 204.

12. Jane E. Brody, "Teenage Risks, and How to Avoid Them," December 18, 2007, www.nytimes.com/2007/12/18/health/18brod.html?pagewanted=1&_r=1&ref=science?_r=1.

13. Ibid.

Chapter 12

1. Alan Guttmacher Institute.

2. The National Campaign to Prevent Teen Pregnancy.

3. Pam Stenzel with Crystal Kirgiss, *Sex Has a Price Tag: Discussions about Sexuality, Spirituality, and Self-Respect* (Grand Rapids, MI: Zondervan, 2003).

4. The National Campaign to Prevent Teen Pregnancy.

5. Millenials Rising: The next great generation, 200.

6. Diana Jean Schemo, "Mothers of Sex-Active Youths Often Think They're Virgins," www.nytimes.com/2002/09/05/national/05SEX.html.

7. Ibid.

8. Hanna Rosin, "Even Evangelical Teens Do It," www.slate.com/id/2167293.

9. Pam Stenzel, *Sex Has a Price Tag: Discussions about Sexuality, Spirituality, and Self-Respect*, 36–37.

Chapter 13

1. Planned UN-Parenthood, January 28, 2008, www.drlaura.com/blog/2008/01/28/planned-un-parenthood.

2. Sex education: Start discussions early, www.mayoclinic.com/health/sex-education/HQ00547.

3. See www.cnn.com/HEALTH/library/HQ/00547.html.

4. Sex education: Start discussions early, www.mayoclinic.com/health/sex-education/HQ00547.

Chapter 14

1. Wendy Shalit, *Girls Gone Mild*, 80.

2. Danielle Crittenden, *What Our Mothers Didn't Tell Us* (New York: Simon and Schuster, 1999).

3. Sharon Jayson and Anthony DeBarros, "Young Adults Delaying Marriage," *USA Today*, USATODAY.com.

4. Ibid.

5. Jeffery M. Leving and Glenn Sacks, posted February 5, 2007, www.enterstageright.com/archive/articles/0207/0207relationship.htm.

6. "Focus Calls New York Times on Anti-Marriage Bias," January 17, 2007, www.focusonthefamily.com/press/pressreleases/A000000694.cfm.

7. "Sex without Strings, Relationships without Rings: Today's Young Singles Talk about Mating and Dating," *A Publication of the National Marriage Project © 2000*, www.marriage.rutgers.edu.

8. Ibid.

9. Glenn Norval, "A Textbook Case of Marriage-Bashing," www.findarticles.com/p/articles/mi_qa3647/is_199805/ai_n8797476.

10. Ibid.

11. Ibid.

12. Danielle Crittenden, *What Our Mothers Didn't Tell Us*.

13. Families and Living Arrangements, Current Population Survey

Reports, Historical Time Series, Table MS2, May 26, 2006, www.census. gov/population/socdemo/hh-fam/ms2.pdf.

14. "Sex without Strings, Relationships without Rings: Today's Young Singles Talk about Mating and Dating," www.marriage.rutgers.edu.

15. Ibid.

16. Ibid.

17. Wendy Shalit, *Girls Gone Mild*, 4.

18. Ibid.

19. Danielle Crittenden, *What Our Mothers Didn't Tell Us*, 66.

20. Ibid.

21. Ibid.

22. Ibid. 74.

23. Ibid.

24. Ibid., 186–87.

25. Dawn Eden, *The Thrill of the Chaste: Finding Fulfillment While Keeping Your Clothes On*, 133.

Chapter 15

1. "Sex without Strings, Relationships without Rings: Today's Young Singles Talk about Mating and Dating," www.marriage.rutgers.edu.

2. Ibid.

3. Wendy Shalit, *Girls Gone Mild*, 19.

4. "Sex without Strings, Relationships without Rings: Today's Young Singles Talk about Mating and Dating," www.marriage.rutgers.edu.

5. Pamela Smock, a family demographer at the University of Michigan, says about 70 percent of those who get married lived together first. "Cohabitation is continuing to grow, and it's become the model way of life," she says.

6. "Sex without Strings, Relationships without Rings: Today's Young Singles Talk about Mating and Dating," www.marriage.rutgers.edu.

7. The National Marriage Project's *Ten Things to Know* Series, "The Top Ten Myths of Marriage" March 2002; Alfred DeMaris and K. Vaninadha Rao, "Premarital Cohabitation and Marital Instability in the United States: A Reassessment," *Journal of Marriage and the Family* 54 (1992):178–90.

8. "Seven Reasons Why Living Together Before Marriage Is Not a

Good Idea," www.stcdio.org/OMFmarriage-ministry/7reasonwhy.htm.

9. "Sociological Reasons Not to Live Together from All About Cohabiting before Marriage," www.leaderu.com/critical/cohabitation-socio.html.

10. Ibid.

11. "Seven Reasons Why Living Together before Marriage Is Not a Good Idea," www.stcdio.org/OMFmarriage-ministry/7reasonwhy.htm.

12. Ibid.

13. Linda J. Waite and Kara Joyner, "Emotional and Physical Satisfaction with Sex in Married, Cohabiting, and Dating Sexual Unions: So Men and Women Differ?" 239–69 in E. O. Laumann and R. T. Michael, eds., *Sex, Love, and Health in America* (Chicago, IL: University of Chicago Press, 2001); Edward O. Laumann, J. H. Gagnon, R. T. Michael, and S. Michaels, *The Social Organization of Sexuality: Sexual Practices in the United States* (Chicago, IL: University of Chicago Press, 1994).

14. The National Marriage Project's *Ten Things to Know* Series, "The Top Ten Myths of Divorce" April 2001. David Popenoe and Barbara Dafoe Whitehead; Unpublished research by Linda J. Waite, cited in Linda J. Waite and Maggie Gallagher, *The Case of Marriage* (New York: Doubleday, 2000), 148.

15. Matthew D. Bramlett and William D. Mosher, *Cohabitation, Marriage, Divorce and Remarriage in the United States*, National Center for Health Statistics, Vital and Health Statistics, 23 (22), 2002. The risks are calculated for women only.

16. J. Wallerstein, J. Lewis, and S. Blakeslee, *The Unexpected Legacy of Divorce: A 25-Year Landmark Study* (New York: Hyperion, 2000), xxvii.

17. Ginny Olson, *Teenage Girls: Exploring Issues Adolescent Girls Face and Strategies to Help Them*.

18. Ibid.

19. Ginny Olson, *Teenage Girls: Exploring Issues Adolescent Girls Face and Strategies to Help Them*, 169; Ann C. Crouter, et al., "How Do Parents Learn about Adolescents' Experiences? Implications for Parental Knowledge and Adolescent Risky Behavior," *Child Development* 76, no. 4 (July–August 2005): 869–82.

20. Wendy Shalit, *Girls Gone Mild*, Fortunately, since 1976 a

nationally representative survey of high school seniors aptly titled Monitoring the Future, conducted annually by the Institute for Social Research at the University of Michigan, has asked numerous questions about family-related topics, 27. Robert Bezilla, ed, *America's Youth in the 1990s* (Princeton, NJ: The George H. Gallup International Institute, 1993).

21. Ibid. Shalit, *Girls Gone Mild.* "Marital Status and health: US 1999–2002," Report from Centers for Disease Control (2004). This study, based on interviews with 127,545 adults age eighteen and up, found that married adults were in better psychological and physical health than cohabiting, single, or divorced adults.

22. "Sex without Strings, Relationships without Rings: Today's Young Singles Talk about Mating and Dating," www.marriage.rutgers.edu.

23. Ibid.

24. Ibid.

25. Ibid.

Chapter 16

1. Jane Lawler Dye, *Fertility of American Women: June 2004*, Current Population Reports, P20-555, US Census Bureau, Washington, DC, 2005, Table 6, cited in *The State of Our Unions 2006: The Social Health of Marriage in America*, The National Marriage Project, July 2006, http://marriage.rutgers.edu.

2. Anonymous, M.D., *Unprotected: A Campus Psychiatrist Reveals How Political Correctness in Her Profession Endangers Every Student*, 89.

3. Kalb, "Should You Have Your Baby," 124.

4. American Society for Reproductive Medicine, *Age and Fertility, a Guide for Patients* (Birmingham, AL: American Society for Reproductive Medicine, 2003), 3.

5. Sylvia Ann Hewlett, *Creating a Life: Professional Women and the Quest for Children* (New York: Hyperion, 2002), 219.

6. Kate Johnson, "Oocyte Freezing: Insurance or False Security?" *Clinical Psychiatry News*, February 2005, 76.

7. American Society for Reproductive Medicine, American Society for Reproductive medicine Guide for Patients, *Infertility: An Overview*, 4.

8. Ibid.

9. A. D. Domar et al., "The Psychological Impact of Infertility: A Comparison with Patients with Other Medical Conditions," *Journal of Psychosomatic Obstetrics and Gynecology* 14 suppl. (1993): 45–52.

10. Sally Wadyka, "For Women Worried About Fertility, Egg Bank Is a New Option," *The New York Times*, September 21, 2004, www.nytimes.com/2004/09/21/health/21egg.html.

11. "I've frozen my eggs so I can have a baby when I'm 60," *Daily Mail*, May 13, 2007, www.dailymail.co.uk/pages/live/femail/article.html?in_article_id=454273&in_page_id=1879.

12. Ibid.

13. Zev Rosenwaks, "We Still Can't Stop the Biological Clock," *New York Times*, June 24, 2000.

14. Sylvia Hewlett, *Creating a Life* (Miramax Publishing, 2004), 217.

15. Ibid.

16. Rick Weiss, "Infertility Campaign Can't Get Ad Space," *The Washington Post*, August 28, 2002.

17. Albert Mohler, "So There Are Limits After All," June 6, 2007, www.albertmohler.com/blog_read.php?id=958.

18. *The State of our Unions 2006: The Social Health of Marriage in America*, The National Marriage Project (http://marriage.rutgers.edu) July, 2006.

19. Ibid.

20. "Is Marriage Becoming Just Independent Roommates with Sex?", August 9, 2007, www.drlaura.com/blog/2007/08/09/is-marriage-just-independent-roommates-with-sex/.

21. Ibid.

22. Helene Flournoy, "Young women picking marriage over careers," April 10, 2007, www.hflournoy@smu.edu.

23. "Choosing Motherhood Over Career? A Trend Among Young Women at Elite Universities," September 22, 2005, www.albertmohler.com/blog_read.php?id=291.

24. Ibid.

25. Danielle Crittenden, *What Our Mothers Didn't Tell Us*, 101–2.

Chapter 17

1. Listen to the executive director of California's National Organization for Women (NOW), Helen Grieco, who recently rushed to the defense of the *Girls Gone Wild* videos: "I think it's about being a rebel, and I don't think it's a bad notion," she told Elizabeth Strickland of the *San Francisco Weekly*. That's because "flashing your breasts on Daytona Beach says, 'I'm not a good girl. I think it's sexy to be a bad girl.'"

2. Mike Straka, "GRRR! Girls Gone Wild," *Newsweek*, February 6, 2007, www.foxnews.com/story/0,2933,250408,00.html.

3. Ibid.

Chapter 18

1. Jeninne Lee-St. John, "Your Own Personal Paparazzi," January 17, 2008, www.time.com/time/magazine/article/0,9171,1704698,00.html.

2. "Study: College Students More Narcissistic Than Ever," February 27, 2007, www.foxnews.com/story/0,2933,254904,00.html.

3. Ibid.

4. Ibid.

5. Merissa Marr, "Disney Reaches to the Crib to Extend Princess Magic," November 19, 2007, www.online.wsj.com/public/article/SB119543097711697381.html.

6. "What's Wrong With Being a Princess? Some Say Girls' Fascination with Princesses Could Be Unhealthy," April 22, 2007, abcnews.go.com/GMA/Health/story?id=3065469.

7. Lisa Nicita, "Generation Diva: Pampering Could Give Little Girls the Wrong Attitude," *The Arizona Republic*, January 15, 2008, www.azcentral.com/news/articles/0115diva0116.html.

8. Ibid.

9. See www.Compassion.com.

Chapter 19

1. Jed Dreben, "The Ousted Idols Have Their Say," March 10, 2007, www.people.com/people/package/americanidol2007/article/0,,2007868_20014697,00.html.

2. James Strong, *Strong's Exhaustive Concordance of the Bible* (Peabody, MA: Hendrickson Publishers, 2007).

3. Arthur C. Brooks, *The Ennui of Saint Teresa*, "On average, religious people are much happier than nonreligious ones," *The Wall Street Journal*, September 30, 2007, www.opinionjournal.com/extra/?id=110010672.

4. Ibid.

5. *The Holman Illustrated Bible Dictionary* (Nashville, B&H Publishing Group, 2003).

6. Merrill F. Unger, *The New Unger's Bible Dictionary* (Chicago: Moody, 2006).